THE Grimmest OF Fairy Tales

Hope Publications, Australia

Hope Publications acknowledge the Traditional Custodians of the land upon which we live & work, and pay respect to Elders past & present.

First published on Wurundjeri Country in Australia in 2025

By Hope Publications

ABN 87 276 858 766

Copyright © Tammy Casselson 2025

All rights reserved.

This work is copyright.

No part of this book may be reproduced or transmitted in any form or by any means, electronic or mechanical, including photocopying, recording, or by any information storage and retrieval system, without permission in writing from the publisher.

A catalogue record for this book is available from the National Library of Australia

Website - www.tammycasselson.com

ISBN 978-1-7640257-0-6 (Paperback)

ISBN 978-1-7640257-1-3 (ebook)

Cover design, Graphics and Typeset by Lucia Sankovic

Author Photograph by Heidi Wernicke, SayHeidi Photography

Printed in Australia

Disclaimer: The events and conversations in this book are accurate to the best of the author's ability, although some names and details have been changed to protect the privacy of others.

Once upon a time, I saw a sign:

One day you will tell your story of how you overcame what you are going through now, and it will become part of someone else's survival guide.
–Author Unknown

I did.
—T. Casselson

For my beloved children, you are my light.
Your love, strength, and resilience inspire me every single day.
Thank you for being my constant source of hope and joy.

To those cherished people whose belief in me has been my
anchor in the storm. Your support, encouragement, and
solidarity has meant everything. Thank you for being my safe
harbour, and my constant source of love and strength.

And, to those who held my hand gently,
even for a moment, listened without judgment,
believed me, and encouraged me to rise.
Thank you for championing me,
for being present,
and for helping me reclaim my voice,
my agency, my power, and my confidence.

Dear Reader,

Within these pages lies my journey, a struggle shared by many, to escape the grip of coercive control. I offer it to bring awareness to this often-hidden form of abuse and as a beacon of understanding and hope.

The contents of this book may activate or trigger difficult and painful feelings. Please reach out to existing supports if you need to. If you haven't yet accessed any support, please contact services listed at the end of this book.

TABLE OF CONTENTS

The Pied Piper: The Charmer	01
Introduction: Bluebeard—Happily Never After	05
Chapter 1: Rapunzel—Isolated for Her Own Good	13
The Red Flags Begin to Surface	15
Understanding Coercive Control and Power Tactics	17
Chapter 2: Little Red Riding Hood—Mr. Perfect Hiding in Plain Sight	23
Understanding the Magnitude of Coercive Control	29
Chapter 3: The Gingerbread Man—Run, Run, Run	31
Courage to Move Forward	40
Chapter 4: Hansel and Gretel—Survival Mode, Treats and Threats	43
Home Is Where the Heart Is	45
Chapter 5: Rumpelstiltskin–Honouring the Truth	49

Chapter 6: Mulan—I Am a Warrior	57
Chapter 7: Cinderella—It Takes a Village, a Fairy Godmother, and a Tribe of Warriors	69
Chapter 8: Alice in Wonderland—A Curious Upside-Down World	75
Spiritual/Religious Abuse	80
Systems Abuse	82
Chapter 9: Pinocchio—The Adorable Liar	89
Chapter 10: The Stolen Farthings—Dishonesty and Disharmony	97
Identifying Features	101
Chapter 11: The Emperor's New Clothing—Grimm Tragedy and Protocols	105
Chapter 12: Goldilocks—Responsibility for our Actions	113
Yellow Rock Communication	116
Chapter 13: Snow White—Kindness Matters	119
Chapter 14: The Little Match Girl—Doing Nothing Does Nothing	125
Panic Attack	129

Chapter 15: The Three Little Pigs—Foundations of Strength	133
Chapter 16: The Tortoise and the Hare—Slow and Steady	145
Australian Resources	152
Financial Abuse Resources	153
Glossary	154
Key Lessons to Share	158
References	165
Sources for Epigraphs and Quotes	169

The Pied Piper

THE CHARMER

The charmer played his music
The men and the women danced
All followed and followed and followed
They watched the pied piper fall
even as he played his music
And they followed and followed and followed
They witnessed the house fall off the cliff
The cars and all he owned
The music was leading to the end
but they followed and followed and followed
The pied piper's family cried out,
the music played on
and the women and men closed their eyes
and followed and followed and followed
Over the cliff the pied piper went
Echoes of music could be heard
The men and the women still danced to his tunes
His family left with the ruins

—T. Casselson

INTRODUCTION

Bluebeard

HAPPILY NEVER AFTER

> *It's doomsday and a call to prayer.*
> —Women Talking

We played pretend by day. I dropped my children off at a private school in the morning, went to my respectable job, and even smiled my way through a number of year-end social functions. Meanwhile, my two children and I were homeless and couch-surfing at night.

Transient. Invisible. Isolated. Stigmatised. Those are not words I'd ever thought I would have used to describe my family. I do not resemble the stereotypical abuse victim. I am well-educated and grew up in a protected, loving, solid, middle-class family. My background is Jewish and South African. I had a great job that I loved and a big circle of friends. I grew up with strong values of respect, love, kindness, family, and education. Few people knew that my children and I were evicted from our home with no warning, had our cars repossessed, and were couch-surfing for over two months.

Even fewer know that for the next seven years, I lived in survival mode, running on pure adrenaline and consumed by panic attacks, nightmares, and anxiety. I lived from one payday to the next, just barely getting through in subsidised housing while frequently attending court, psychologist appointments, and lawyer visits. And, more frequently, you'd find me at police stations, trying to make sure my children and I were safe.

There are over 122,000 people experiencing homelessness on a given night in Australia. (Australian Bureau of Statistics, 2023). I had no home address. My body was numb, my brain full of fog, and my panic was building daily.

My story has many similarities with numerous I have heard, including homelessness, huge secret debt, stalking, children and religion being weaponised, threats to safety and livelihood, a broken court system, paralysing fear that my ex was coming to kill me and/or my two precious children, and police who mostly ignored my fears and sent me away.

The Grimmest of Fairy Tales tells my story, showing that intimate partner violence can happen to anyone from any religion, any educational background, any profession, any community, any ethnicity, and any income level. No one is exempt.

This story also shows the confusion around intimate partner violence and coercive control. I only understood I was in an abusive relationship after leaving that relationship. I knew it wasn't good, but until I had an understanding of family violence, I didn't understand what I had been living with. You may be wondering how that is possible. This book explains the confusing tactics a perpetrator uses.

There is a myth about what a victim of family violence looks like. The fact is it can happen to any of us. It happened to me. None of us are immune. A 2021 National Community Attitudes Towards Violence Against Women Survey (NCAS) showed 91% of respondents agreed violence against women was a problem in Australia. However, only 47% agreed it was a problem in their own community (Coumarelos et al., 2023).

MYTH	FACT
Only physical violence is family violence, and it is the most damaging.	Emotional violence, psychological violence, financial violence, and religious violence are incredibly harmful and devastating. The consequences are life-changing, disempowering, and trauma-inducing.
Women make false claims and exaggerate abuse.	Women are more likely to downplay abuse, and 80% of abuse goes unreported (Safe Steps, 2014).
Women would leave if it were so bad.	The research shows that the most dangerous time for a woman is when she is pregnant or when she talks about or attempts to leave (Safe Steps, 2014). This is when she is at the highest risk of violence, including murder. She has often been threatened and intimidated, and just a look is enough to make her go cold with terror.

While this is my story and my lessons learned, my co-author and friend, Anastasia, has been a huge support in writing this book. She has also helped add a different lens, explain and reframe some concepts along the way. We hope this book reaches out to you as friends, neighbours, allies, survivors, or possibly people going through something similar right now. We want our book to offer help, hope, lessons learned, expertise, and experience. A big message is that transparency is equally as important as trust in the foundation of a relationship. We also want to highlight the importance of equality in relationships to allow for growth and longevity.

I believed I was in a loving partnership. In reality, there was deception, fraud and betrayal for most of my marriage and for the years of post-separation abuse after I had escaped.

While Anastasia and I are Australian, this is a universal story and message. I have heard stories and met victims and survivors from around the world, and many who have inspired me have become close friends. The statistics are staggering. The fight is surreal in its familiarity. The pain is indescribable. Healing and growth are achievable. Connection across the world builds strength.

We all need to be emotionally and financially literate. To be empowered, all parties must have access to banking and financial information and understand their financial position and the decisions they are making in a marriage or partnership.

Society and systems must help us create transparent processes and ongoing information chains. That includes joint visits to lawyers, financial advisors, insurance companies, and banks for informed decision-making. Laws and policies for lawyers, insurance companies, banks, and financial investors need to change. The systems and society we live and work in need to know how to better assist survivors and how not to become co-conspirators with abusers by leaving openings for abuse and misuse.

We hope to destigmatise intimate partner violence (IPV) for victim-survivors. There is huge shame and silence around IPV, and it is most often unjustly placed on the victim and not the perpetrator. It is the perpetrator who chooses their behaviour. They choose to be charming and engaging to magnetise people towards them. They also choose to be violent, threatening, manipulative, and deceitful with the victim. The shame is on the perpetrator. We need to hold the perpetrator accountable for their behaviour.

IPV is a societal issue, and we all need to work to stop it. We all have a part to play. We can choose how we make a difference. We hope by reading this book, people will understand how to reach out to women and men they think may be in potential danger, listen, and offer allyship.

We hope victim-survivors will read this book and feel hope that healing and growth are ahead. We explore recovery and healing options and offer reassurance that healing is not a linear process but is attainable.

We also discuss the prevalence of coercive control (specifically financial, emotional, and religious) and post-separation abuse. We explain how you can be an ally and a friend and how this can mitigate the secondary trauma survivors endure when they are not heard, believed, and supported. Choosing to do nothing, be neutral, and making jokes enables the abuse.

This book highlights how dangerous a perpetrator can become when you attempt to leave or actually leave. The worst years for me were the seven years post-separation. I was sure

I would be killed, or my children would be killed. I explain how I kept us safe while creating a loving, happy home for my children to thrive in. We can be two things at once: afraid and brave, sad and happy, protective and empowering, or grieving and celebrating.

I was married for 20 years. The seven years post-separation were the most difficult, incredibly long years of growing, learning, fighting, and finding a tribe of warriors who keep me sane, loved, calm (most of the time), inspired, knowledgeable, and laughing. I have always believed that we constantly learn and grow, and when we know better, we can do better. I also believe my purpose is to teach, guide, and inspire. I want to be able to use my pain, growth, and learning to help others create better awareness and gain greater knowledge, skills, and tools to feel empowered if they must themselves face or help someone through a similar journey.

By working on letting go of "people pleasing" (still an ongoing process) and letting go of the need to be understood, it got easier to find my voice. Finding my voice was my journey. It may not be yours, and that is OK.

ONE

Rapunzel

ISOLATED FOR HER OWN GOOD

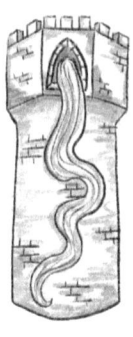

The limits of my language mean the limits of my world.
—Ludwig Wittgenstein

Long, long ago, in a land far, far away, a smiling, happy-go-lucky girl (me) met her Prince Charming. I can't begin to describe how handsome and intriguing he was. He wore an Air Force uniform and the cutest, cheekiest smile. He had a playful way, and he broke the rules, something I never did. He made everyone swoon with his good looks, magnetic personality, and confidence. He was the adored baby of his family on whom everyone doted. He had been at a boys' school and was the cool kid with a huge group of friends.

It was 1989, and I was 15 years old and smitten. My heart melted when he told me I was special. My Prince Charming treated me like his princess, his "happy-go-lucky" girl. Gifts, attention, affection, promises.

Prince Charming was a real knight in shining armour. He seemed to jump to my defence, noticing danger and protecting me from it. He was proud of me and spoke about my achievements as if they were his own. He called me many times a day, flooding me with attention, and he sometimes followed me to check I got places safely when he couldn't escort me there himself. He very quickly became central in my life and a constant in my family home, having used his boy-next-door innocent charm, good looks, and wit to woo my family. He made them laugh at his jokes and fall in love with him too.

We started a bank account together before we were even engaged. He said we would save together for holidays, a home, and a life together. We planned a future. We bought one mobile phone together when they first came out (a brick!). I carried it around, and he called me on it often to check in.

I dreamed of a white princess wedding dress, the white picket fence, the giggling baby, and a husband who adored me. I dreamed of love and cuddles, building sandcastles on the beach, and watching our children grow as I held hands with my Prince Charming.

THE RED FLAGS BEGIN TO SURFACE

I saw the red flags. I thought it was a carnival.
—Author Unknown

When I did things he wasn't included in (like university events), he would get really grumpy and miserable, which would escalate to outbursts. These outbursts began a few months into our relationship. Very occasionally, he became very angry and explosive, then it was all over and done. Once, he told me to get out of the car on the highway. I did. He yelled, "Get back in." He was super possessive of me, "his girl."

Every happy occasion—parties, my 21st, my matric dance (formal), or my graduation—seemed to result in me in tears at some stage. I tried to make him happy by doing things his way and we lived happily for the most part.

When things were good, they were super good. We laughed and had fun. We went on adventures. Things certainly looked picture-perfect. The sometimes-grumpy, sometimes-charming man made sure we—and later, we as a couple and our two dimpled, well-mannered children—were always a "happy family" to anyone watching. Picture-perfect.

Over time, little red flags kept appearing. I, now a young woman, mostly-smiling-and-making-the-best-out-of-life, would make excuses for the red flags. Of course, sometimes it was a survival strategy—just managing the red flags. I sometimes perceived them as red roses (completely misunderstanding they were flags). Sometimes I knew they were flags, but I thought they would pass. "It's stress." "It's anxiety." "He is overwhelmed." "He will eventually get help."

He went to get medication. Nothing changed. He was erratic. He was manipulative. He made huge gestures, huge promises, then huge threats. I was constantly on edge.

We were married for 20 years. The last 10 years were very stressful. The fairy tale had slowly become a horror story. My knight became my captor. He would fly into a rage because I didn't answer him quickly enough. I still didn't have the words to explain what was happening. I couldn't make sense of it. My body felt it. I got sick. I had visits to the hospital. Stress exacerbated my symptoms.

He would tell people of his daily arduous visits to me in the hospital, but in reality, it was a 10-minute, cold visit where he checked my file and said unkind, mean things to me. He was happy with me being heavily medicated and in hospital. He was furious if the doctor suggested stress as a factor or the need to talk to a therapist, and even more angry if a therapist or doctor spoke to me while he was not present. My friend, a social worker, commented that he wasn't very nice to me. By now, I, only-sometimes-smiling-but-mostly-anxious, made more excuses for him.

"Prince not so Charming" became a scary devil. He looked at me, a sad, terrified woman, in a way that made me shrivel up. There were threats from him that I had better not leave him. Threats that things would get much worse if I did try to leave him. There was so much confusing behaviour as a sad-anxious-trying-to-survive woman I didn't know what was true or real.

Now, as a not-smiling-at-all-woman, I was not allowed to go out with my friends. If I did, I would be punished for doing so. I was repeatedly told I was not enough. Many of my movements and decisions in my day were controlled by my not-so-wonderful-man-become-devil (sometimes small and insignificant, sometimes big and life-altering). I was unable to trust anyone, including, most importantly, myself. As I felt less able, less capable, and less trustworthy, I became more dependent on him.

Besides all the control, threats, and stress, there was huge amounts of ongoing, concealed, underhanded behaviour that I, the always-on-edge-trying-to-protect-her-children person, never even suspected was going on in the background. I would only find this out later.

UNDERSTANDING COERCIVE CONTROL AND POWER TACTICS

I was unaware of coercive control for many years. The term was only officially defined in Evan Stark's 2007 book, *How Men Entrap Women in Personal Life*, as "a pattern of behaviour which seeks to take away the victim's liberty or freedom, to strip away their sense of self" (Stark, 2007).

Coercive control includes a repeated pattern of dominating behaviour in a domestic relationship (some form of long-term companion relationship). This dominating behaviour is controlling and restricts the other person's freedom and independence. Coercive control can include verbal, financial, psychological, emotional, sexual, and physical abuse. Coercive control most frequently continues (often escalating in danger) as post-separation abuse, including systems abuse, when the victim-survivor attempts to leave the relationship (*Coercive Control*, 2020).

Dr Emma Katz defines coercive control as involving "situations where a person causing harm subjects another person/s to persistent, wide-ranging controlling behaviour over a long period of time, behaviour that goes beyond the reasonable expectations that people have of each other in families and relationships, and makes it clear that standing up for themselves will be punished, i.e. 'do what I say, or else…'" (Katz, 2023).

Coercive control is often difficult to describe or even to identify. It's often not even seen as abuse because it is such a manipulative, insidious process. There is second-guessing, complete dependence on the abuser, punishment and reward, love/ trauma bonding, violence, or the threat of violence.

I had no way to explain what was happening or describe the confusion. I had no voice. Even after our split in 2016, our friends were blinded by the charismatic charm of my ex. How often do we hear stories of men who abuse or even kill their spouse being called "good men" or "good fathers"? People have a difficult time believing what they have not seen, even when evidence is presented to them.

He played the victim and spun stories. He told friends I had abandoned him in his time of need. In his version of the story, he had been a great father and husband who was destroyed by the terrible wife who left him because he was depressed, and she told his children horrible things about him.

If I had known about coercive control or if it was a criminal offence, I would have been more aware, educated, and possibly behaved differently. Perhaps those friends who enabled his abusive behaviour may have known better and may have behaved differently too. I may have spoken up to more people. I may have shared my concerns with more people, and I may have escaped earlier.

Often, the coercive relationship begins at a young age. I was 15 when he began with these behaviours. Coercive control is the repeated pattern of controlling behaviours causing harm over a period of time:

- Putting rules (control tactics) in place early with consequences for stepping outside.
- Allowing me very little time alone with friends (alienation).
- Checking in wherever I was (*control*).
- Becoming easily jealous of other relationships.
- Forcing the end to any relationship deemed threatening.
- Pushing to pick fights with family members (manipulation).
- Making phone calls to me all day, every day (*stalking*).
- Threatening me.
- Doing surveillance under the guise of checking to see that I was OK.
- Making promises. Breaking promises.
- Issuing more threats.

- Putting me on a pedestal in public and boasting about how wonderful I was, including my accomplishments as a student, as a wife, in my career, and as a mother. In private, he insulted me and broke me down (gaslighting).
- Yelling at any little mistake: a dropped avocado pip, using too many pots and pans to cook a meal, being too messy when I baked, or me offering to do a favour for a friend.
- Using punishments and rewards.
- Promising holidays. Cancelling holidays.
- Splurging on jewellery and then telling me there was no money for professional memberships I needed for work or shoes for the children.

The perpetrator uses subtle techniques to groom both the controlled and the people around the controlled to trust and love them. In *See What You Made Me Do*, Jess Hill (2019) explains how the process is very similar to that of the grooming process of a sexual predator. My family loved my ex. He had grown up in my family home. He was charming and caring and a "good father." So, to try to get my family to consider another version of him (one they had never witnessed) was very difficult. Their only reference was the façade of Prince Charming.

We need to break down these myths:

The Monster Myth:

- We know what an abuser looks like.
- Perpetrators are monsters, and we will be able to spot them.
- It only happens in other communities.

- We would have known.

The abusers live amongst us, hidden in plain sight. If we could easily identify the perpetrators life would be much simpler:

- If we knew, we would not date or marry them.
- If we knew, we would not die. Our children would not die.
- If we knew, we would not have millions of dollars of debt we knew nothing about.
- If we knew, we would not be homeless with two teenage children.
- If we knew, we would not allow them to break our self-esteem and make us feel worthless.
- If we knew, we would not continue to protect them as they spread lies about us.
- If we knew, would we stand by the perpetrator rather than the victims?
- If we knew, would we stand by and do nothing?

LESSONS I HAVE LEARNED:

- Abusers do not look like monsters.
- Victims look like your neighbours. Like me. Like you.
- Education is key.

TWO

Little Red Riding Hood

MR. PERFECT HIDING IN PLAIN SIGHT

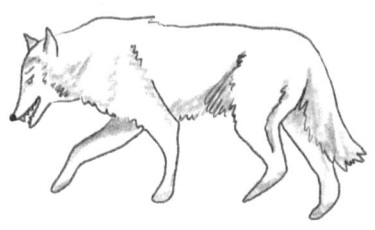

For me, it was a fairytale turned horror story.
How do you fall for the Devil?
You don't.
You fall for Prince Charming.
—T. Casselson

Kindness became taunts, cuddles became disaffection, love became disloyalty, trust became fear, and my dream became my nightmare.

I very slowly began to awaken as I realised the sad-feeling-locked-in-and-very-alone woman I had become and realised I had to break out. In 2016, I began challenging him for information about our banking. I knew I needed access. I still had no idea of the looming debt or years of deception I was about to uncover. He became angry and more restrictive. The man-become-devil-monster escalated his threats and harmful behaviour.

And suddenly, the world crashed down. Ground zero day: 19 October 2016. Secrets became exposed, and while it seemed like this was the biggest threatening disaster, for me, stunned, scared to death, having gone into survivor mode, it may have been something utterly different... This was my chance to escape.

For years, I told my ex that I was "wearing his stress." I couldn't have been more correct. I was physically and emotionally holding his stress. My energy was being drained. I showed physical symptoms of stress that came out as chronic illness and fatigue.

After the first 10 years of marriage, as things deteriorated,

I stayed, hoping things would improve. I encouraged him to get medical and psychological help. Eventually, I began to try to refuse to absorb his energy and tried to put up boundaries to protect myself. I would tell him his behaviour was not OK and that he could not say those things to me. I'd tell him he needed to please be kinder and please apologise. He would never apologise. This only made him angry, and he would escalate his control, threats, and meanness. My children had noticed there was an issue the year before and asked him to get help. It was at this point I knew I had to get out. I had no idea how to do that, and moreover, I realised I had no access to any financial resources.

Even after all these years, I had no idea the depth of the situation I was in or any realisation of how long I had been in a controlling relationship. I had no idea the man I had been with for more than half my life had been lying to me and deceiving me for most, if not all, of our relationship. I had no idea that the pattern of ongoing threats he used, his campaign of confusion against me, and crying often were all part of the same suite of symptoms of emotional abuse. I had no concept that my abuser, by not allowing me access to any financial information or accounts, had a means of power over me and used that power to control and abuse me (restrict, exploit, and sabotage me) throughout our marriage and for years after.

It was only on ground zero day and over the following months that the enormity of what was going on in my house revealed itself. On this day, I found my husband near death and began to question whether he would follow through with some of his threats. On finding him, I dialled emergency services in complete disbelief that he would ever attempt to hurt himself. He had threatened me. I believed he would hurt me—but never himself. It was only when I got home from the hospital hours later, still in shock, that I looked next to his bed, in his drawer, and found a big bag of credit cards that I had never seen, some with my name, some with his. There was a tower of unopened and opened envelopes on the floor. Overdue accounts and an eviction notice. We were being told to leave our home immediately. Our cars were being repossessed. There were five mailbox addresses he was using simultaneously. Our children's bank accounts were empty. All their savings had been paid to creditors.

It was financial devastation. I had lost all security. And for my children, at such a crucial time in their development, one of their primary relationships of trust was completely shattered. I worried not only for their financial safety but also for their psychological safety. Both of my children had been so vigilant in saving all their money for years.

My son had been working incredibly hard to save for a car and an overseas trip with his friends as his high school career culminated. For my daughter, the breach was incredibly destabilising. Her lack of agency at that time spoke volumes. This passionate, headstrong, independent, goal-directed, determined, natural leader I had always encouraged to speak up was stunned. She was now told that all decisions she had made with great financial responsibility were abused, and her opinion did not count in the eyes of the law.

School fees for both children were long overdue. Friends, family, banks, and loan sharks were owed huge amounts of money. Calls, texts, and emails came in for months (and, in some cases, years) as more debt was revealed, and my ignorance became confusion, disbelief, and horror. This had been an ongoing process many, many years in the making. Ten then fifteen years of evidence slowly showed itself. This was a well-thought-out pattern of deceit.

We had been fighting for a few months by this stage, but I didn't know anything about the incredible amount of debt. I had picked up a tension. I could feel something was not right. I hadn't been able to look at him. I had realised I had no access to any banking, including any online banking and had just been demanding some form of access to money.

After his attempted suicide, I sat in the psychiatry ward with a team of specialists, including a psychologist, a psychiatrist, and a social worker, as they explained to me that he had a narcissistic personality disorder. There is a spectrum of narcissism. He was showing enough pathological signs of the traits to be labelled as narcissistic. Narcissism is characterised by an inflated sense of self-importance, a craving for excessive admiration, and a lack of empathy for others. They often believe they are superior to others, exploit relationships for personal gain, and have difficulty acknowledging the feelings or needs of those around them. Narcissistic individuals tend to be arrogant, boastful, and demanding, expecting special treatment without justification (Mayo Clinic, 2023).

I asked the specialist team if something was cognitively wrong with him and if he had known what he was doing. He kept making the same decisions. They all agreed: there was nothing cognitively wrong with him. Nothing damaged. In fact, he was choosing this behaviour. That is an important distinction. A mistake you make over and over is a choice. A choice he made when he told my daughter it was her fault that he tried to "kill himself because she didn't love him" and my fault because I overspent. A choice he made when he explained the details of his long-thought-out actions to two traumatised children. A choice he made when he lay in hospital yelling commands at me and continued illegal financial transactions from his bed. He could control his behaviour in front of others. He chose not to control it in private.

Five months before this suicide attempt and us reaching ground zero, I wrote an email to him after a particularly threatening fight:

17 May 2016

X you are unstable and you need to get help. Your daughter is scared of you, your son asked you to get help and I am begging you.

What will it take?

Should I call your brother? Your father? My father?

I can't handle it anymore.

I have to protect my children and myself.

Go to the doctor, change your meds and see a therapist. I understand you are under immense stress. That does not give you the right to scare Y [daughter] *or put me down or break us all down.*

Get help. I'm begging you. You are destroying all of your relationships.

When you yell at me for something completely out of my control and put me down in front of the children you are making my condition worse and alienating your children. You have to stop. Just leave me alone. Please.

He flew into a rage when he saw this. He said people had access to his work email. He called me disgusting names. He sped off to work to delete it. When he came home, he was still furious. Pacing. I was silent. Petrified. The fear settled in. He made threats. I lay on the bed. Closed my eyes. Stayed very still.

UNDERSTANDING THE MAGNITUDE OF COERCIVE CONTROL

97% of intimate partner homicide is preceded by coercive control. (*New South Wales Domestic Violence Death Review Team, 2022, p. 28*).

According to the Australian Bureau of Statistics (2023):

- One in five Australian adults have experienced violence, emotional abuse or economic abuse by a partner.
- With women more likely than men to have experienced violence, emotional abuse, or economic abuse by a partner since the age of 15.
- Just over 1 in 4 women experienced partner violence or abuse (27 percent or 2.7 million women)

If you could tell by looking at someone that they were an abuser, intelligent, empathic, kind men and women would not be getting into these relationships to begin with.

It is happening ALL around you in every community.

We need to listen better. When people speak out, we need to acknowledge them. We need to believe survivors.

LESSONS I HAVE LEARNED:

- Abuse happens in ALL communities.
- Listen, acknowledge and believe survivors. Violence is a choice.

THREE

The Gingerbread Man

RUN, RUN, RUN

Freeing yourself was one thing, claiming ownership of that freed self was another
—Toni Morrison

There had been whispers long before the louder warnings. They became shouts before the universe brought a deafening, horror-film-sized scream.

The person I first met at 15 was loving, funny, handsome, helpful, and so charming. He was long gone, but I held hope that he would return. We had always been together, and I believed we would always be together. My parents had modelled that marriage had difficult and good times, and you just stuck with it. My parents taught us that you committed to something. I have always seen every job through. I stuck with doctors, therapists, hairdressers, coaches, and a husband for much longer than I should have, from a sense of responsibility, honour, loyalty, and a need to be conscientious. I believed things could get better. This is known as escalation of commitment: sticking to a decision even when the feedback tells us it's time to change directions. This is why it is so important to listen to the whispers of our gut instinct.

I had tried suggesting we split amicably in the years preceding 2016. We were both so obviously unhappy with each other. When I said our marriage was over, he warned me over and over how ugly it would get. There were many, many threats. This, I have learned: It is not about going out with our friends. Or how we parked the car. It is not about how many pots and pans we used to cook the meal or who we smiled at in the grocery store. It is not about where the children go to school. It is not about custody of the children. It is not about child support. Everything is about power and control.

There were threats before leaving and so many more threats after. The more he felt power and control slip from him, the more his behaviour escalated. I felt increasingly scared the more out of control he felt and completely petrified and fearful for my life and my children as I got stronger and gained more agency.

Ground zero day, 19 October 2016, when I found my abuser slumped over his desk, and the days after the attempt were mostly a blur. The whole tower of our pretend-perfect lives came tumbling down. Our marriage, our home, our belongings, all security, and the father figure gone. Discovery of his betrayal. So much betrayal. Years of betrayal. Over a million dollars of debt in my name. More in his name. Everything crashed down in a huge, messy explosion, and yet I felt a deep sense of obligation and duty to my childhood love, the father of my children. I was stuck in this very heavy sense of duty. I now understand this as trauma bonding. After his first suicide attempt, the team at the hospital (psychologist, psychiatrist, social worker, doctor), as well as the team at the rehabilitation facility, told me to stop visiting him every day.

He was still abusing me. Carrying out financial transactions. Withholding information and access to financial accounts. From his hospital bed, he was saying threatening, hateful things to myself and his children. They made a decision not to visit him. It was completely overwhelming to be around him. I would take him to Centrelink, for example, and he would yell abuse at me all the way there, sit there being abusive, and yell abuse all the way back. Threatening me. Threatening my children's wellbeing. There was so much fear. Fear and anxiety.

All consuming. My stomach in knots. My head pounding. I felt frozen. Escaped but still chained by a sense of responsibility.

In my case, I didn't recognise it as abuse or coercive control until after I had left the relationship and was able to understand the emotional and financial abuse I had been living with for years. I had great difficulty putting into words what I was going through; I couldn't understand it, so how could I begin to verbalise it? I was a victim of gaslighting.

It was a slow education.

I remember a day in court in early 2017 when I looked down, and among the documents was an "abuse wheel" diagram in the middle of the table. This is a common framework used to explain control and power:

- Using Intimidation
    - Glaring at me in a way that I knew meant he was going to hurt me, punching his fist within millimetres of my face.
- Using Coercion and Threats
    - Threatening to kill me or himself or the children or all of us.
- Using Emotional Abuse
    - Calling me names, telling me I was worthless, or that I was dead to him.
- Using Isolation
    - Controlling when I could go out and punishing me if I spoke or saw people.
- Minimising, Denying, and Blaming
    - Not accepting responsibility for his behaviour, saying I made him do it, or denying it had even happened.

- Using Children
  - Telling the children I was abandoning them, smashing their favourite items, and threatening to hurt the children.
- Using Male Privilege
  - Making sexist jokes and getting others to agree with his role as the "boss" or reprimanding me.
- Using Economic Abuse
  - Not giving me access to banking accounts, signing documents in my name, accumulating debt in my name, and giving me an allowance.

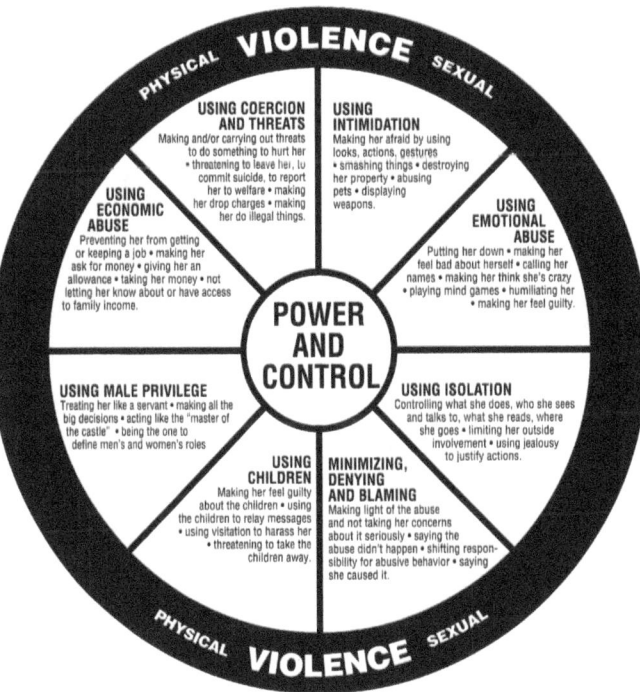

Copyright by the Domestic Abuse Intervention Project 202 East Superior Street, Duluth, MN, 55802 218-722-2781

This was my situation. I was a victim-survivor of domestic abuse. Of intimate terrorism. It is a similar story that I have heard from other survivors. A moment of surreal, sick realisation.

A real awakening moment and a big shout-out from the universe was in 2011, five years before the cyclone hit us. My best friend was dying from a very aggressive, incredibly quick-moving cancer, and I sat at her bedside, first at home and later in the ICU. My friends and I watched as she slowly left us. We saw her say goodbye to those she loved most. We stayed by her bed or sat in the doorway, and we felt her slip away. My mind was numb, and my soul and heart were sore. It was a privilege to be with her. She was full of grace. Always.

I watched as my friends' husbands embraced and consoled their wives. Meanwhile, my husband was only cold and furious with me. He was enraged that I was spending hours away from home. He told my children (7 and 12 years old at the time) that I was "abandoning" them. He yelled into the phone and called me names. Instead of offering me support and love, he would constantly say, "I am going to start saying Kaddish for you—because you have died." (A Mourner's Kaddish is said by Jewish people in memory of someone who has died.) And in those few days, I not only lost my best friend, but I also lost my first love. My sweetheart was gone forever. He had shown slivers of himself, but never had he shown me this level of cruelty or this complete lack of care or empathy. He would never acknowledge his behaviour or apologise for it. He would only escalate his nastiness and abuse if I mentioned it. "I" was to blame. "I" pushed him to behave like this. For me, our relationship was over.

When he behaved like this, I asked him to move out. I told him this was the end of us. He threatened that he would never accept that. We would never be over. He did not apologise. I heard only repeated threats from him: "I am grieving. My wife is gone. If something happens to me, you will regret it."

I tried to reason with him. I begged him to get help. I said to him, "You are not behaving rationally. The medication will help you feel better. This is not an acceptable way to behave. You can't say these things over and over. This is not you. Can you not hear how sick it is to say these things when our friend has just died?"

His response was anger.

Swearing.

Bullying.

More threats.

Fear. Anxiety. Panic.

He kept repeating that I had abandoned him and the children.

More raving.

More aggression.

Then accusations. He told me I was mentally unstable.

I go out with my friends too much.

I am a disappointment as a wife.

I'm so tired. I'm so sad.

He tells me that if I allow a clean slate, all will be OK.

Exhaustion.

Deep sadness.

Escalation.

I am making him sick.

If he dies, it will be my fault.

Alarm.

Disbelief. He would never hurt himself.

If you leave, you will see what happens to you. The children.

I believe him.

A whole-body anxiety reaction.

You will see what will happen if you leave me. It will get very ugly.

Fear. Desperation.

Panic.

The confusion is so difficult to explain. The rising fear and anxiety. The desperation and the feeling of being stuck in a situation and completely isolated. As I explained before, it is such a mind-fuck that you don't know what the truth is.

And, of course, with hindsight, everything is so clear. Many whispers are so easy to hear. So many red flags waved to me for so many years. I was so young and looked at the world with rose-coloured glasses. I am an incredibly trusting human, such an optimist. I love life. I live with the hope that everything will turn out right.

I ignored some red flags as I did not understand their consequences, while others I was completely blind to. Some red flags I hoped would change over time; some red flags I recognised and begged for action to be taken.

A few red flags I see in hindsight include:

- He believed that rules didn't apply to him at school,

in the army, or at work. He found a way around them.
- He had a general disrespect for most people. He called old people "oxygen thieves" and could never get serious about death. He had no empathy at all on the subject. He could however fake empathy really well.
- He was incredibly possessive of me and my time.
- He needed to be with me and check in with me constantly. I misread this as care, concern and love- it was control.
- He phoned me several times a day to check where I was and who I was with.
- He controlled his angry outbursts—especially at the beginning of our relationship, but when he did lose his temper, it was big and loud.
- It was always my fault.
- There was never an apology. There was escalation if I showed any sign of being upset at his behaviour or asked for an apology.

When he was unwell, he was incredibly demanding and unkind. When he lost his licence for six months and I had to drive him around, he was rude, dismissive, and abusive. No one should get away with treating another person in a demeaning, dehumanising way. There are no excuses.

What is clear is the importance of raising our awareness of red and green flags. The empowerment that knowledge brings. What does a healthy relationship look like? The result will be connections and relationships that are strong, positive, healthy, and mutually beneficial.

Also, the more knowledge we have, the stronger our intuition becomes, and the more we feel we can trust ourselves.

Our intuition is our superpower. We need to learn to tune in. Mine has never steered me wrong—when I was listening. That can be as easy as taking a breath, being in silence, and then trusting ourselves to listen to our inner voice.

We need to know it is OK to leave when it is right and safe for us. Many of us come from a belief system that we are failures if we leave a relationship. We are told we need to persist and keep trying. I had tried for years. I had begged him to get therapy with or without me. I had begged him to try medication. I had begged him to stop behaving the way he was. I was hopeful he would change. I believed the kind, attentive man I had once known would find his way back. I have emails and letters that I sent him. Our children begged him to get help. He could never see a problem. He could never acknowledge he was doing anything wrong. He could never apologise.

COURAGE TO MOVE FORWARD

As I sat in that meeting in 2016 at the hospital, being told he was narcissistic and of sound mind, after my world had collapsed around me, I saw my opportunity to escape. I worked with his team to decide when and how it was best to tell him.

We need to accept we cannot heal or fix anyone else. We are not responsible for anyone else's happiness. And it's healthy to choose a different path. To start again. To pivot.

LESSONS I HAVE LEARNED:

- Trust your gut. Your intuition is your superpower.
- Trust your inner voice, your inner wisdom. When people show themselves, believe them. Hear the whispers. That's the real person—RUN!

FOUR

Hansel and Gretel

SURVIVAL MODE, TREATS AND THREATS

The wolf's charm is most potent when it circles its prey

I knew my ex could be incredibly unkind to me. He often used the technique of reward and punishment. I had to watch carefully and step in to protect my children. On occasion, this behaviour would extend to them. More so with my daughter, including name-calling, spoiling special days, and breaking precious items.

On one occasion, in 2014, he destroyed a truly remarkable experience for her. I was devastated. She got a position in *The Voice Kids* Top 100 with a friend. It took many tough (and fun) audition rounds to get through to the Top 100. The girls were chosen because they were feisty, cute, and had the sweetest little voices. We—the two mums and two girls—were offered a trip to Sydney for a week. The girls were beyond excited. A clothing chain sponsored them with a whole week's worth of matching outfits. They were given a few coaching classes, and we thought they sounded terrific. Mostly, they were just a lovable, endearing, cheeky, and funny duo.

My ex was miserable and acted out throughout this process. He was offended and angry that the mothers were invited and the fathers were not included. He accused me of doing something or saying something so they excluded him. He began to get nasty. He informed us he would join us in Sydney. I asked him not to come. He arrived halfway through our time there. The girls had been having so much fun up until this point. He made us uncomfortable from the moment he arrived. He made me cry. He made her cry. This incredibly fun opportunity became about him.

The girls didn't get the judges' chairs to turn. They did get to hang out with an incredibly talented group of kids for a week. They sang songs constantly, felt like celebrities, and had a fabulous time. They got to meet the judges, got huge hugs from them, and, of course, a great photo. That gorgeous memory will always be marred by the cruel comments, tantrums, and self-centred behaviour of her father.

Just before everything came crashing down in 2016, my son had a horrible "car-dooring" incident. He was about to write his final school mathematics exam. He had one more year of school. He had been working 20-hour weeks, studying and cycling to keep fit. He was knocked off his bike on a busy road while riding home from work. His bike was damaged, his smartwatch was broken, and his hand needed stitches.

The money that the driver of the car and road trauma insurance paid to fix the bike "disappeared." My son never had his watch repaired, and I eventually paid for the bike repair.

These were little erosions of trust, unexplained and never apologised for.

HOME IS WHERE THE HEART IS

My children were 12 and 16 when we became homeless. We packed our bags and, for two very long months, slept on various cousins' and friends' spare mattresses. I had to swallow my huge pride and accept supermarket vouchers and money from our community. We had no car. People were incredibly generous in lending us theirs. The days were day-to-day living, adrenaline-pumping, and confusion-filled.

Ashamed I hadn't seen what was happening in front of me, grateful to have my children near me, confused as to how

I reached this point, and terrified of each new day, I tried to stand solid so that my children believed the world was steady.

My abuser told people I "abandoned" him and that I was "alienating" the children. He left out of his story that while he refused to pay child support, he tried to bribe his children with trips or payments if they saw him. While he stripped their bank accounts and then threatened them, he told the court it would be best for <u>his</u> mental health to see the children. He never once mentioned what was in the children's best interests.

There is nothing that excuses abuse. All abuse is abuse. Emotional abuse destroys people. It crushes your confidence and your self-worth. Emotional abuse leads to severe physical and health problems, including chronic pain and anxiety.

LESSONS I HAVE LEARNED:

- Children are victims in their own right.
- Children's voices need to be heard.

FIVE

Rumpelstiltskin

HONOURING THE TRUTH

Mastery of language affords remarkable power.
—Frantz Fanon

"Why don't they leave?" "Why didn't you leave earlier?"

Our society is focused on the victim. Our spotlight should be on the perpetrator. For so many reasons, these are the wrong questions to ask. Instead, we should reframe the questions: "Why didn't he let her leave?" "Why did he abuse her?" "He controlled his behaviour with others, so why did he choose to behave so abusively with her?"

Our system is filled with emotive language:

- "The boy next door"
- "The stand-up bloke"
- "Just one of the guys"
- The police talk about a "deserving victim"

Other derogatory terms get thrown around, like "victim mentality." When people refer to this person who has been and is still being abusive, a popular term used is "a good father." How are those congruent? How can a man who is emotionally and/or physically and/or financially abusive to the mother of his children as well as the children be a good father? Another popular term is that abusers are referred to as having been "upstanding citizens and successful." If he was abusive, was he then upstanding?

Until coercive control becomes criminalised in every state of Australia and every country, reporting breaches of intervention orders is useless, and we are not seen as "deserving victims." We are not the "ideal victim." Instead, the message you hear is, "They have not broken the law. Come back when they really do something."

On 1 July 2024, coercive control became a criminal offence in New South Wales, Australia. The maximum penalty is up to seven years imprisonment (New South Wales Government, n.d.). It has also been criminalised in England (2015), Ireland (2018), and Scotland (2018). In the USA, there is pressure to make coercive control illegal. Many states, e.g. California, Hawaii, and Connecticut, have already included coercive control as a form of domestic violence or abuse.

There is a problem of misidentifying victims versus abusers. The abuser taunts the victim for so long that they often provoke the victim to act. When the police arrive, the abuser is speaking clearly, has their story together, blames the victim, and even plays the "victim" perfectly. Meanwhile, the "real" victim is traumatised, stutters, can't string their words and sentences together and seems psychologically unstable. They seem to be the problem.

I have heard some devastating stories of victims losing their children to the abuser because of misidentification. I have had women sobbing while telling me their stories. I have walked the depressing halls of the courthouses watching broken women and men hunched over as a system informs them they will break the law if they do not hand their most precious children over to their abuser.

Abusers know how to stay just inside the lines.

Seven years post-separation, my abuser was still using accounts with my name that he had not disclosed. He was paying debts off to chosen friends but refusing to pay child support. His lawyer was sending threatening letters daily, and he became a vexatious litigant, filing a colossal number of never-ending court applications with no substance. My ex admitted in open court to breaching intervention orders and coming within inches of me, and yet there was nothing that could be done other than to extend the intervention order.

These are the added problems that an already broken, overloaded system needs to deal with. Correction to the system begins with trauma-informed education for all court officials, police officers, and anyone coming into contact with either the victim or abuser.

Court and legal systems have historically been patriarchal and not trauma-informed. A trauma-informed approach ensures doing no harm and creates a safe environment that will not re-traumatise victims. It is a system that works with victims to empower them rather than continue to remove agency from them.

The court talks about "high conflict cases." This makes it sound like survivors are equal participants or are there by some sort of choice. It is a high abuse case. My abuser dragged me through the system for seven years. The emotional and financial cost and the impact on my health were immeasurable. Intimate terrorists will do everything to deny you rest or peace. For example:

- They will frustrate and abuse the legal process and create reasons for you to return to the courts or police.
- They will find ways to torment the healthy parent through the children, school, child support.
- They are looking to hold onto any control over you and and will use any means that will allow them to punish you.

When my teenage son got to spend time with men in our

community they pressured him to see his father, prioritising his father's best interest above my son's feelings and lived experience.

These men should have stood up, spoken up and been positive role models for my son, not reinforced my ex's behaviour.

Parents do not have rights. Children have rights. Parents have responsibilities.

Each time we went to court, my ex would use the same argument. How important seeing the children was to his mental health. To his wellbeing.

The judge, the psychologist, and the psychiatrist wanted him to see what was in the children's best interest.

If he engaged in therapy, that would have been a step forward. If he acknowledged his role in the actions he had taken, there would have been accountability. Unfortunately, he couldn't or wouldn't do that.

Our society, the community, journalists, and counsellors do it too. In abuse situations, "it takes two to tango" is not always true. "There are two sides to every story" is destructive. Society and systems become complicit in that abuse when they use this language. We need to be outraged. We need to call it out. It is time for all good people to speak up.

What the survivor needs to hear is "I hear you" and "I acknowledge your pain." What they hear from you is a discounting of their truth. The abuser's story is that they are the "victim" in the scenario.

I will be clear here in stating that we are all responsible for our own behaviour. This is not a book of finding blame or settling scores. Rather, it is a book that hopes to guide others and give people language to use that I did not have. We only do better when we know better and when we choose to do better. The abuser in my story chose to make the repeated decisions he made and continued to show no humility, apology, or change in behaviour. Most abusers don't. As for others who got caught up, most were victims, too, of the grooming and manipulation of this man who used them as enablers to defend, minimise, and sometimes even cause pain themselves.

The abuser understands how to get others to go along with his berating and emotional battery. Other men may think they are "bantering," doing the old "boys being boys" thing. For the abuser, this is an opportunity to gaslight, gang up on, and embarrass his partner in public. The humiliation, put-downs, and breakdowns of self-esteem allow for questioning of truth to occur. Later, the abuser is able to use those conversations as evidence. The abuser is a master at manipulating perceptions of self and the situation. This leads the victim to lose trust in themselves and depend more on the abuser.

Sometimes it is subtle, and sometimes it is obvious to all. Most often, nobody calls it out. It's time to break this cycle. My abuser would do this with a close group of our friends. He once tried to get our friends to gang up against me about an accident I had. He was frustrated when they said, "That's why it's called an accident" and "It is only a car." These responses deescalated the discussion and validated me. He would also do this with my family. Often, the joking escalated the stress. "Women are difficult." "Women are impossible to please." We need to call this out. Role model respect.

Not all disrespectful behaviour is violent, but all violent

behaviour begins with disrespectful behaviour (*Coercive Control, Non-Physical Violence and Relationship Red Flags*, n.d.).

Nothing excuses abuse. Emotional abuse has profound negative impacts on a person.

The abuser uses many techniques. The definition of love, for example, in some cultures, is that of dependence, attachment, complete trust, and entitlement. For example, gendered roles around financial management might apply.

We need to have an awareness of what emotional abuse looks like to identify it and to know it is unequivocally not OK. We need to have safe spaces to share our stories where we won't get judged so we can begin to understand and develop coping and life skills. What are we modelling for our children? We need to include children as victims when we discuss domestic abuse and intimate partner violence.

We are all responsible for building a society where we listen with compassion and curiosity, not judgement. One where we listen to, acknowledge and support each other. One where no one has agency over another.

LESSONS I HAVE LEARNED:

- Believe women.
- Listen, acknowledge and support when people come forward.
- Believe victim-survivors when they tell their story.
- If it's safe, we must try to be upstanders.

Six

Mulan

I AM A WARRIOR

Trauma does not make us stronger; it does allow us to discover our inner strength.

—T. Casselson

One of the most crushing aspects of abuse is the sense of isolation. Escaping, only to find yourself alone and unheard, unacknowledged, and in some cases even disbelieved, is incredibly painful.

What it does do is make you fiercely independent. I learned I had to depend on myself. I learned about an inner strength I hadn't known existed before.

This is a common thread I find in discussions with other survivors.

More aftershocks of my world falling apart came when people who I thought I would be able to depend on were not so dependable. People who let us down. Who turned out not to have the strength to face the truth. Who didn't want to face the possibility of abuse in "their family" or in "their community." Who refused to believe the children over the adult. Who stood by the abuser. Who broke promises to me. Or who said the right things and then didn't follow through, leaving me even more helpless.

As exhausting as this has been, and as much grief as this has brought, my mission was (and remains) solid. My values too. To protect my children. To feed, clothe, and educate them and help them be the best they can be. To use each day I have to find joy, hope, and kindness for myself and others. I make a conscious choice not to let other people's behaviours impact my behaviour.

We spent seven years returning over and over to court. The children made it very clear to their father what they needed: for the threats and games to stop. They wanted him to get help. He would refuse to pay anything towards our household, school clothes, or books, and then offer overseas trips to the children. He would send texts and letters of love and then break all the relationship rules by breaching trust and asking friends, the school, and sports groups for the location of the children.

He would strain relationships with charity organisations that were assisting us, threaten friends and organisations who helped us, swear at a Rabbi, and make demands on the school supporting us. Anyone offering us help or kindness was open to his threats and abuse.

This was one letter of many sent by my lawyer to my ex, trying to get the behaviour to stop:

> *With regards to your continual harassment of ▇▇▇ accounts department, please refrain with immediate effect from any further communication with the school.*
>
> *As you know, the intervention order against you forbids you to be in contact with anyone who causes emotional stress to myself or ▇▇▇ This is doing just that.*
>
> *As you well you know, I have made an offer to you before the conciliation conference, at the conciliation conference, in front of the registrar ▇▇▇ and today again in front of Chief Judge ▇▇▇ whereby I stated that I am prepared to take over the whole school debt and indemnify*

you of same.

I would like to remind you that the judge stated today in court that "you appear to not be acting in the best interest of your children."

Should you continue to harass the school, I will be forced to report you to the police for breach of your intervention order.

Tammy

Some of the closest people in my life did not want to hear that I had been betrayed in every way possible by this man I had trusted my entire adult life. Not only did they not want to hear, but they chose to make excuses for his behaviour and support him rather than support me and our children.

There were so many complex components in the midst of trying to stay calm and grounded for my children. My son was in the final stages of his intense and stressful school years. He had worked so hard and set high goals. I wanted this to be a memorable time for the right reasons. My daughter needed order, peace, and security after all she had been through. And, of course, they both needed lots of love and a reliable parent they could depend on and trust. That was my main focus.

I was trying to deal with life's practicalities: opening a bank account I could have access to, finding two homes (one for the children and myself and one for my abuser), cars, ensuring secure schooling, getting access to and paying bills I had never paid, going to work as if everything was fine, discovering and sorting through millions of dollars of debt I had never heard of, and then facing the shame of my perfect family crumbling.

And where to begin with the imperfection and taboo

subjects: mental health issues including suicide, depression and personality disorders, financial collapse, family violence ("not in our community"), homelessness, separation, and divorce.

At first, I tried to explain to a select few. Truth is, people hear what they want to. When I confided that I had had to get a court order to keep my abuser away from my children and me so that we could feel safe, I had a "friend" tell me she doesn't trust the courts. She continued to support him and did not believe there was abuse. I had a "friend" tell me I needed to take over the debt my abuser owed him because even though he had promised my abuser that he would NOT disclose to me about the debt, he told me he would not have lent my abuser the money if he had not been told it was for me.

While people could see my ex's vulnerability, that his mental health was fragile, they could not see that he also chose to deceive those closest to him. They could not see through the manipulation. When I'd attempt to speak to attitudes perpetuating this behaviour, I'd hit a brick wall. Some people remained closed to changing their own behaviours and mindsets.

A person close to me told me that if the way he "bantered" made me uncomfortable and triggered, that was too bad because that was the way he grew up and that is how he talked. I had "close friends" prefer to show support to an abuser, entertaining him and inviting him to celebrations, rather than to support myself and two young teenagers whom they knew he had emotionally and financially abused. This isolated us further. There were those who pushed for the children to see the abuser. "He's their father." "We never saw him do anything wrong." "Did the children contact him for his birthday?" "Did he physically hurt the children?"

> *We must always take sides. Neutrality helps the oppressor, never the victim. Silence encourages the tormentor, never the tormented.*
> —Elie Wiesel

We tell women to leave. Society pressures women to leave. We make women feel ashamed and guilty for not leaving or not leaving sooner. Are there enough systems in place to protect women when they leave? We know that intention or preparing to leave and separation are when women are at their greatest risk.

Psychiatrists, social workers, police, and lawyers all warned me. I was offered counselling. It wasn't enough. I was terrified he was coming to physically harm or possibly kill us. He had threatened many times. I stayed awake at night. I had panic attacks. Would I be the next Rosie Batty? Rosie became a well-known Australian family violence campaigner after her son Luke was murdered by his father in a public assault. Would my worst nightmare come true, and my children be killed one day when I wasn't there to protect them? Or would I be the next Hannah Clarke? Hannah Clarke was killed by her estranged husband in a murder-suicide along with her three children, aged 3, 4, and 6, in Queensland, Australia, in 2020, after she had repeatedly reported him to the police. So many horrific stories.

Would he kill all of us together? Or would it be me he killed? Could he access a gun? Only I had ever seen his potential for violence. The fear was real.

He tried constantly to communicate. Disgusting, demanding, degrading emails, texts, and calls. Constantly. Hundreds of messages a day flooded in. He stalked me and my children. He sent texts to our then 12-year-old daughter:

> *Father: "i'm coming to netball"*
> *Child: "Please don't"*
> *Father: "u can't stop me"*
> *Father: "what r u going to do call the police"*

As he escalated, his rage got more out of control. The less control he had, the crueller and more vicious he became—more threatening, more angry, and more scary.

He assaulted me. On one occasion, he got so angry, he was yelling words of abuse and brought his fist up and almost slammed it into my face. His fist stopped millimetres before my nose. He didn't need to hit me for the impact to have an effect. The near impact caused enough pain, terror, and intimidation.

The fear and panic were overwhelming. I was sure he would make contact. I wasn't sure what would happen next. The threat was enough. The terror was enough. He knew he was back in control.

One night in 2017, he pounded on my apartment door. Fear. Anxiety. Apprehension. My daughter and I asked and then begged him to go away, both of us in tears, trembling, and sweating. I called my son and told him not to come home.

I told my ex over and over to please leave or I would call the police. He shouted back, daring me to call them. Terror swept through me. Flashbacks to other occasions. Panic seized my brain. I heard him call his lawyer, who advised him to wait for the police. Instead of helping the situation, the lawyer further escalated things. My daughter and I heard him pacing outside. He kept shouting the abuse. My daughter was sobbing. I was begging for him to leave.

The police arrived.

His demeanour completely shifted. He played the calm ex-partner and caring parent who had come over to deliver a gift. He explained I was the overly emotional woman making my child neurotic.

The police asked him to leave. He left.

Court documents show my daughter told the court-appointed psychologist that on that day she was "terrified."

A safety assessment is done. It goes nowhere. Without laws against coercive control he is not breaking the law – yet.

I was finally pushed to take out an intervention order.

In the story he tells he is the victim just trying to visit his daughter with gifts.

I am the crazy ex keeping him away.

His friends feel very sad for him. Maybe even encourage him. His friend, the psychiatrist, fuels him further by explaining that I am 'alienating' him from his daughter.

His lawyer enables his behaviour.

These enablers, have been used by the abuser as tools, as a means to an end. Firstly, the abuser knows that by using them, it will further antagonise the victim. Secondly, the common manipulation technique of playing the victim is a form of isolating the victim further and reinforcing the victim script. By choosing the abuser over the victim, you actively become an accomplice, and if you are not actively doing it, you are not facing up to the damage you are inflicting and the good you could be doing. You are not looking at the big picture and the innocent children who need to be seen, loved, and filled with compassion. Good people can do bad things. We can do better. Learn better and do better.

"Flying monkeys" is the term given to the active helpers of the narcissist. In my situation, these "helpers" included:

- The brother who, on behalf of the abuser, wrote abusive letters to a nephew he should be protecting. When the teenager tried to explain that the father refused to pay child support, was going on holidays, living well, and the children and mom were in subsidised housing being helped by charities, the brother wrote, "You are jealous of your father that he is doing so well."
- The friends who protected the abuser from any legal action being taken against him and spoke out actively against the protective parent keeping her children safe.

There were many moments that felt like aftershocks of the earthquake that shattered our life as we had known it. All these little aftershocks and ripples that told me I was alone and needed to step up and take control. I had to be my own warrior, fight for my children and myself, and work it out. There is an inner strength in all of us.

There is a reflection to add here. This deep feeling of isolation becomes a keen need for independence which can lead to a difficulty in letting others in or allowing others to help you out. We become so fiercely protective of our newfound agency that we push people away. We need to remind ourselves that we build connection through sharing and vulnerability and that it is OK to be both the helper and the helped at times.

While part of our healing is learning to let people in again and accept help, please keep reaching in and offering support and kindness. While our instinct is often to retreat, every kind word and gesture means more than you will ever know.

LESSONS I HAVE LEARNED:

- Post-separation experiences with friends and family may be complex and can perpetuate abuse because some people choose to refute your lived experience, not acknowledging they too had been manipulated.
- Let people in. Independence is important. So is connection when you feel safe to do so.
- Keep reaching in to check on people – compassion, kindness and connection are the keys to recovery.

SEVEN

Cinderella

IT TAKES A VILLAGE, A FAIRY GODMOTHER, AND A TRIBE OF WARRIORS

We are hurt in connection, and we heal in connection.
—T. Casselson

I have adapted an old story about an egg, a carrot, and a coffee bean. When we have been through terrible pain and trauma, we get to make a choice—although often, we don't know it. We believe we are broken and scared and feel as if the grief and wounds will swallow us up. We have three choices: to be a carrot, an egg, or a coffee bean.

The carrot, the egg, and the coffee bean are tested by being placed in boiling water. Each reacts differently. The carrot becomes soft, weakened, and fragile. The heat breaks it down. The egg becomes hardened, solid and stiff. The subjection to heat removes its softness. Finally, the coffee bean opens up and releases its flavour and aroma. The coffee bean remains intact in the heat and brings about change.

This is a metaphor for our experiences through trauma and adversity. We can choose to grow around our pain, scars, and grief. It may, in fact, always be a part of us. It may knock on our door of consciousness and peek in from time to time, but we can still choose to live with joy and purpose around it.

Do you want to weaken, harden, and become closed off, or choose to be solution-focused and open-hearted, and to live holding onto hope?

Part of healing is taking agency for your life and story. Often, survivors feel they have to explain themselves. A common theme is oversharing or freezing and not knowing where to start. I think it's important for survivors to know it's OK to not tell their stories. It can be a protective, survival, healing boundary we set up. We all have different coping mechanisms, and we get to choose what works for us in our own time. We have no control as victims; we can have control as healers. We can set boundaries. We can choose how we share, what we share, with whom and when we share it.

We can also be vulnerable and authentic without sharing.

There is a time for everything.

There were friends who questioned me for not sharing my story earlier. They felt 'hurt' I hadn't shared what I was going through. In discussions with many survivors, I have come to know this to be a common thing for victim-survivors. There are many reasons victims don't share:

- There can sometimes be competing motives, where friends can see the power and the benefit in you sharing your lived experience but may not be aware that the timing may not be right.
- It may not feel safe to share.
- We feel shame or fear that our story isn't believable.
- We may have received threats.
- Victim-survivors may not recognise themselves as victims of domestic violence until just before we leave or after we have escaped (Hill, 2019).

I know that it is not risk-free to be a coffee bean. I know that it is not an easy road. I do know that we will all have days of being carrots and eggs, but I wish more courageous coffee bean days for us all. I do know for sure that it feels so much better to be a coffee bean at the end of a long day. I do know that there are some special people who will gravitate towards you and make it easier to be a coffee bean. I do know that if you choose to be a coffee bean, you will inspire others. Bravery inspires bravery. And we all need bravery.

Please know that we are all connected.

Please know today will pass.

Please know I see you, I hear you, and I believe you.

What a survivor needs to hear is that they have been heard. That their story has been shared in a safe space. That you acknowledge their pain. If someone reaches out and shares their sacred story, listen, acknowledge, and believe them.

And for survivors, please know part of healing is finding your voice. It takes time (sometimes years) to be able to verbalise your story. It is also a very painful process to share bravely and to have certain people react differently to how you hope they will. (And this happens to all of us—I have spoken to so many survivors.) There is a shock that comes when you realise that people doubt you, and instead of offering compassion and understanding, they offer judgement or disbelief. There is a great loneliness in this and a huge amount of grief that gets added to the already huge amount of shame, grief, and sadness you are feeling.

My advice is to take the process slowly. You decide who to share with and how much. Make contact with professionals first. Speak to counsellors and therapists. Share your story only if and when you choose to.

Finding your voice goes against a victim's self-preservation instinct because for so long you've been brainwashed that you don't matter and that no one will believe you. There is a deep knowing of the consequences of revealing what is under the façade. Part of healing includes sharing our stories in safe spaces. Freeing our secrets. There is a physical, spiritual, and emotional release.

I had so much grief to process. A broken dream. Life as I knew it was over. And I grieved for some of my dearest friends. I was devastated that they chose to support my abuser and controller rather than my innocent, beautiful children, who needed all the love and guidance they could get. I knew how we had surrounded and supported friends who had lost partners and was shocked that my children and I did not get that same care and consideration.

I was blessed to be a part of other communities who did embrace us. Who nurtured and mentored my children. Who loved and cared for us.

LESSONS I HAVE LEARNED

- Feel your emotions. We have to feel our emotions, and all emotions are valid.
- Grief comes in different forms, and we have to honour our grief process.
- Talk to people who listen, acknowledge, and support you. Reach out to people who listen and acknowledge your pain and your story.
- Reach out to resources available. There is help out there. We've provided a list of resources at the end of this book.
- Get counselling.
- Let go of those people who no longer support you and your journey, as difficult as that is.
- If you want to support victim-survivors, make them feel heard and listened to.
- Ask what support they need.

EIGHT

Alice in Wonderland

A CURIOUS UPSIDE-DOWN WORLD

Escaping did not mean the end of abuse. It was just another more confusing chapter, a different form of terror, control, and cruelty. The panic sat firmly on my chest. I can remember the first day I faced my abuser in Melbourne Family Court in 2019. In the build-up, there were so many threats, so much intimidation, harassment, and stalking. I no longer recognised this man. He was a stranger. His posture had changed, and his face looked different; it was tight, angry, mean, threatening. How could I know him so well and also not know him at all?

Years of visits back to court, filling in countless forms, documenting and retelling my story. Thousands of dollars wasted. Endless interviews by court officials, psychologists, psychiatrists, lawyers, social workers, school teachers, financial counsellors, financial institutions, police, judges, more judges, and more lawyers. Visits to police stations, courts, and charities, and then online court days. I faced my abuser endlessly as he dragged the processes out, bringing me back to court over and over, watching as he played "victim."

I had to take the stand and endure aggressive questioning by his equally abusive and disrespectful lawyers. Abusers hire abusive lawyers who are disrespectful to survivors when cross-examining them. His lawyer called me a "liar," a woman who "abandoned her suicidal, depressed, helpless husband," and a woman who "alienated" her children from their "loving, good father."

It would be very nice to say we have a fair and just legal system with ethical lawyers. Unfortunately, that is not my experience or the experience of most people I have come in contact with here in Australia or in my network overseas. The system is very broken, with many people working to try to fix it—many wonderful lawyers, police, and court officers. However, there are many people not fit for the job taking advantage of the system while people are hurting. Ruthless lawyers, "puppets," attempted (and sometimes succeeded) to provoke me, doing anything to win points. I experienced fear, shame, grief, anger, sadness, exhaustion, overwhelm, and then the same over and over.

Everything I did was with the aim of keeping myself and my beautiful children safe, always reminded by my children to add little sprinkles of light, joy, hope, and love to each day.

On one occasion, 5 February 2020, a day we were in Melbourne Family Court, my abuser used his lawyer to snigger at me in court and call me a "liar."

What is ironic is that the court was on a short break because we were waiting for bank statements that I had subpoenaed to show that my abuser had hidden funds he had not disclosed to the court.

He did it again. "Liar."

My strong sense of justice switched into gear, and I felt like I left my body. (disassociation) All the pent-up rage that had been frozen in my throat came tumbling out loudly. I started yelling in court, at the lawyer, and at my abuser. I didn't ever look at him. I was too afraid. I usually sat quietly between my calm, strong, confident lawyer and my protective, concerned father, who was always at my side. But I was a woman possessed. All my emotion flooded out as I screamed that I wasn't the liar but that he was. I kept screaming about the hidden money, the stolen money, the lies he told, his deceit. I wasn't a liar. He was.

I watched the court security guard move towards me.

I kept yelling. I couldn't stop. My abuser had deceived and cheated in every way possible.

My father moved towards me. The court security guard moved towards me.

My abuser just sneered at me. It was the reaction he had wanted. I became silent. I would not behave like that again in front of him.

But I had found my voice.

I liked it.

An abuse story that really stayed with me was a woman who said her abuser had been emotionally abusive until the day she left. (As I have stated before, the most dangerous time for women is when they show intention to leave or when they leave.) As she was leaving, he punched her hard in the face. She said she was so grateful for the bruises.

I sobbed when I heard this. The sadness really overwhelmed me. Firstly, sadness for her. Secondly, for me. She had such a terribly hard time. She was grateful that she had been taken seriously as she sought help and was treated with respect and kindness. People believed her.

My sadness for myself and others without visible bruises was that we are often turned away, not believed, and not treated with kindness and compassion. People do not see the deep wounds. If only we could show the bruises on our hearts and souls. How would we be treated then?

I have been at the police station reporting for myself and with others who needed to report and been told to "come back when something serious happens" or treated like we were wasting the police officer's time. At other times, we were treated with incredible dignity by empathetic police officers who were determined to help in a very broken system.

Once, my ex took me to court for noncompliance with a family order, an order that my daughter was to see a psychologist. I had been engaging with a psychologist for both my children and myself from as far back as my ex's first suicide attempt. I am a strong advocate for therapy. The family order was such that sessions needed to be paid by my ex, before each session, and he was refusing to pay. My ex was not paying anything else for the children. No child support. No school fees. Nothing. I had to cancel an appointment very late as it was unpaid. I was still taken to court for not complying with the order. I was forced to miss work. I was forced to face my abuser and a courthouse, which were huge anxiety-provoking triggers for me. I was forced to engage a lawyer to defend me.

The judge threw out the case, dismissing the complaint.

There were multiple court visits where my ex tried to have my daughter removed from her school, where she was loved, protected, and thriving in all areas. Again, control and power were the drivers for my ex; anxiety and fear were the results for me. And, of course, time and cost. Cases were always thrown out of court, but this did not make the stress any easier to bear.

For me, his inability to prevent himself from being provoked was my one silver lining. Each court-appointed social worker, psychologist, counsellor, or court-appointed lawyer who attempted to cross the narcissist in him was hit with the same self-important answers. He wanted to see the children for *his* "mental health." He breached the orders because he "wanted to." He had gone from "zero to hero" because he was "working three jobs" and "earning $120,000 a year." He walked into their traps.

He would walk out of court having signed an agreement not to contact the children and then send a text to them before I had even informed them of the outcome. A psychologist, a policewoman, and a lawyer all informed the abuser that his daughter did not want contact with him, but the texts, emails, and letters persistently arrived. Breach on breach on breach. Police would go over to his residence and warn him, discuss this with him and he would do it again.

All this behaviour, while draining and anxiety-provoking, was also incredibly helpful. The chief judge said, "You do not seem to be acting in the best interests of your children," and "You seem incapable of listening." Over and over, my abuser was denied access to the children in court. And that was all that was important. Keeping them safe. He refused to sign papers for a renewed passport in front of the court-appointed independent children's lawyer. His goals and need for power were transparent to the decision-makers.

SPIRITUAL/RELIGIOUS ABUSE

Intimate Partner Violence and Post-separation abuse can include spiritual/ religious abuse. For me this included refusal to give a religious divorce, leading to court proceedings. In the Jewish religion, both parties must be willing to agree to the religious divorce, called a gett. Without the dual acceptance of the divorce, there is no divorce. If you do not have a gett, you are an 'Agunot' or 'Agun' (male), meaning 'chained'.

This is a gendered issue as the consequences for a woman

are much greater than for a man. As a woman, any future relationship you have with a man is seen as an extramarital affair. If you do choose to remarry civilly, you will not be married under Jewish law. If you have a child, that child is deemed illegitimate and is not considered Jewish. The same does not apply to a man. He can have relations and remarry and have children with another woman—with no consequences.

I am not a rule-breaker. I am not religious. I am, however, deeply spiritual. I had been deceived by this man in every way possible. I did not want to be chained or connected to him in any way. I did not want to die with my soul chained to his. I wanted my liberty. My agency. I had been controlled and silenced for most of my adult life. I wanted to be free. I wanted to be able to find love when I was ready.

I joined Unchain my Heart (a Melbourne based Australian organisation created to eradicate the existence of chained women) as an ambassador, and they advised me how to use the Australian laws which recognise gett refusal as "an example of overt exploitation and unconscionable control that constituted a form of family violence" in the Magistrates Court of Victoria. It took two years of fighting, with my abuser sending abusive, threatening emails to me, my lawyer, and the Rabbi of the Beth Din (Jewish Religious Court). I had to spend money I did not have and exert strength I did not know I had, but I was no longer an Agunot. I was free.

Prenuptial agreements have proven to be the most effective solution to date for couples seeking a swift and amicable gett process. These agreements outline the terms of a gett should the marriage fail.

SYSTEMS ABUSE

Post-separation abuse included my abuser getting a subpoena for my daughter's psychology session notes. To demand notes from therapy sessions where a child is talking in a safe, confidential space is a giant breach of trust and confidence. The most important bond a parent has with a child is security, love, and trust. He broke that bond constantly, never acknowledging the damage he was doing.

There is no accountability for abuse. Taking all the children's savings out of their bank accounts was devastating to them. He told them it was to pay their expenses, and he blamed it on them. He refused to take responsibility for his actions or to apologise. The children's bank accounts clearly show payments made for his business and for repayments on loans for that business.

He always put himself first. He maintained I "alienated" the children from him. He blamed his mental health problems on them. He tried to bribe them (offering rewards and money, gifts, and trips), but when that didn't work, he threatened them. He maintained constant contact via calls, texts, and emails at their workplaces and schools. When they asked for no contact, and it didn't work, he'd reach out to their friends. Another breach of trust and the intervention order in place.

In court, my abuser was asked to characterise our daughter. He was asked if she was fragile. He said, "Definitely not. She is determined, strong-minded, academic, and knows what she wants." That is, in fact, a correct assessment. My daughter is fiercely independent, strong, caring, and determined. He was then asked if he could see the contradiction. He was accusing me of alienation, of "coaching" her, and yet saying she was strong-minded, intelligent, and determined. She knows she has a choice and access to a phone. Even the judge agreed in summation.

Often, the narcissist will accuse you of doing what they are doing (projection). He had tried to discredit and estrange me by telling the children I was abandoning them anytime I was not present.

DARVO, meaning "deny, attack, and reverse victim and offender," is a term used to explain how an abuser turns the story around and becomes the victim.

Jennifer J. Freyd wrote about DARVO in 1997 as a part of "betrayal trauma theory." She explained DARVO as "a reaction [that] perpetrators of wrong-doing, particularly sexual offenders, may display in response to being held accountable for their behaviour" (Harsey & Freyd, 2020). The abuser reverses the roles of victim and offender, becoming the perceived victim and the victim to the offender. You only have to listen to what their accusations are to know what crimes they have committed.

This is an example of how abusers turn things around. How women are often wrongly identified. I have sat with crying women who have lost custody of their children to men who have abused them because the women appear "hysterical" and "unhinged." The abuser is calm and collected. They point at the women and show the evidence of "a woman with psychological issues." (Of course, this can happen to men, too, but the evidence shows it happens to women far more than men.)

This is more frequently found in Indigenous communities,

where we see a high percentage of women being taken into custody. Police arrive (after being called by neighbours), and the victim-survivor begins to talk incoherently. (They are traumatised and afraid for their and their children's lives.) Often seen as "bad victims," mistaken as the perpetrators of the violence, they are jailed and lose their children to the abuser. They and their children often lose their lives.

Examples of horrific cases include Tamica Mullaley and her son, Charlie, in Western Australia in 2013, and Jody Gore, as well as so many more.

In March 2013, Tamica Mullaley and her grandfather, Ted, were treated as criminals and suffered traumatically at the hands of police as her son was taken by his abusive stepfather. Her grandfather was arrested for trying to help Tamica. Charlie was found a day later, horrifically and fatally injured. In 2022, the Western Australian government apologised for the "unthinkable" grief that Tamica and Ted have had to endure.

On 13 June 2015, Jody Gore was in a fight for her life. Her ex-partner, who had been drinking, physically assaulted her. She fought back. She believed he would kill her. During the fight, Jody used a vegetable knife to stab him once in the chest. Both her ex-partner and Jody collapsed from injuries and were taken to hospital, where he died. Jody testified to a 20-year relationship of violence—physical and verbal. A 12-person jury rejected that Jody acted in self-defence.

The judge sentenced Jody to life in prison, with no parole for 12 years. No representation was given to Jody. No witnesses were called on her behalf to prove a domestic abuse situation.

Four and a half years into her sentence, the Western

Australian government chose to show "mercy" and compassion that had been missing from the trial. Jody was granted parole.

One thing that I've heard more than anything else is "there is no justice." For someone who has always held justice as a very strong value, who always followed the rules and who has been beaten and hurt so completely, it is incredibly crushing to hear. There are so many roadblocks. Police who cannot do anything when you sit crying and explain the panic you feel. Lawyers who can only focus on the smallest, silliest details. Laws that protect abusers. Financial institutions that enable the abuser. Courts that give out an interim counter intervention order without even checking facts. (This is an intervention order when there is an intervention order already in place against the person now bringing the complaint—often called vexatious.)

In my interim intervention order case, I was not present. I did, however, get a copy of the judgement recording. The judge did not listen to the application; he only asked my ex if the allegations that he was making against me were true. The allegations my ex had listed included:

- "The respondent used to scream at me all the time."
- "The respondent has been emailing every day in relation to our financial settlement."
- "The respondent encouraged my daughter to make a speech against me."
- "The respondent used false allegations that I stole money and that I am suicidal."
- "The respondent tarnished my name."
- "The respondent denigrated me."

The judge awarded an interim intervention order. For me, that meant money, stress, anxiety, and facing him again, a long, drawn-out process.

The speech in question was to raise awareness and funds for a community charity that had offered us housing, financial counselling, and psychological support. My daughter was asked to make a speech and include her lived experience. No names were used. She wrote it herself. I was so proud of her for her strength, resilience, and ability to give back. Her courage was inspirational. She spoke about us couch-surfing when we were made homeless and her father's attempted suicide. She mentioned him taking her money. All of this was public knowledge. She spoke about achieving great things in spite of her circumstances. This was all true, and it had a huge impact on her. She spoke of the incredible assistance we had. Beautiful comments of support came from the audience.

The next day, threatening legal letters began to arrive for both me and the community charity, demanding public apologies. A day later, lawsuits were threatened against me and the charity. After a week of constant harassment, which I ignored, the intervention order was presented. By the time the court date, which had been postponed and continued, finally arrived, my abuser had strengthened his story. He said the speech had made him suicidal, that I had coerced my daughter to make the speech, and that I had written it and coached her. He called a work colleague/friend (his favourite flying monkey) as a witness, stating I had coached her. This is a friend who has never said more than a passing hello to my daughter or me and hasn't seen my daughter or me in years. Flying monkeys are commonly used by narcissists to do their abusive work. Under oath, this flying monkey said I was "alienating" the child from their father, with nothing to back up the claim.

When my lawyer tried to question my abuser, he said the questions were making him feel emotionally unstable and suicidal. He could not answer any further questions. The judge said he was done being questioned.

I was told I was gagged. A two-year intervention order. For my ex's mental health, I could not speak of my experience of abuse for two years. My lawyers said we could appeal. We could go to a higher court. More money, more stress, more anxiety, more contact with my abuser. I declined. I lost any chance of using my voice. Systems abuse. System failure. More post-separation abuse.

Post-separation tactics include:

- Counter-Parenting: Sabotaging the other parent's role by imposing conflicting rules or withholding essential care for the child.
- False Accusations of "Alienation": Using unfounded claims of "parental alienation" to deflect blame from abusive behaviour.
- Neglectful or Abusive Parenting: Exposing children to harmful environments or individuals through neglect, intimidation, or manipulation.
- Isolation: Intentionally damaging the victim's relationships with family, friends, and support networks. Spreading rumours, destroying reputations, and compromising support systems.
- Harassment and Stalking: Using persistent and frightening tactics to control and intimidate the victim.
- Legal Abuse: Exploiting the legal system to gain power and control over the victim.

- Financial Abuse: Withholding or mismanaging financial resources and support to maintain power and dependence.

LESSONS I HAVE LEARNED:

- For gett assistance, see https://www.facebook.com/unchainmyheartaus and Cheirut International.
- Court systems and processes can sometimes be misused by abusive partners to perpetuate domestic violence. Making choices about whether you proceed with claims should be based on how safe and able you feel at the time. Agency and safety are very important.
- Post-separation abuse is used by abusers when they feel they are losing control over their ex. The abuse from within the relationship continues and often escalates post-separation. This is how the abuser can hurt and punish the healthy partner/parent.
- We need stronger laws in place to deter perpetrators. We need to have coercive control criminalised. We need financial abuse criminalised. If we want women to feel safe enough to leave, we need systems in place that support and protect them. We need systems to re-skill and re-empower them.

NINE

Pinocchio

THE CHARMING LIAR

Actions reveal character—not words.
—T. Casselson

From my early years, I remember my father teaching me that "perception is reality." That we all take the world in differently and that our perception is our truth. So truth then is relative. At what point in my 30-year relationship did things change? I will never know which percentage of the days were spent with a charmer who loved me and which percentage was spent with a charmer who was trying to hide things from me.

In a relationship where one party was a fraud and duplicitous, using you as a pawn in his games, were any perceptions of joy, love, and happiness real? If one of you was genuinely in a partnership and loving and believing in a future while the other was cheating and lying and imploding, what reality existed? If there was no partnership or love, would your experience of joy disappear? When you find out there has been deceit of every kind in the most central, most important relationship of your adult life, you question any feeling of love and connection you had.

Thirty years of fun, dreams, laughter, and excitement got wiped out. Each incident of tears, fear, sadness, and meanness became a focal point. I analysed memories and reinterpreted red flags I could have used as warning signs long before my life shattered into a million tiny shards. Regret, grief, and shame engulfed me so that I had to remind myself a number of times a day to breathe.

The grief of losing the life you and your children know is one thing. The grief of losing the future you imagined is another. The grief of all that you did not and will not experience. And then all the grief of those wasted years. Wondering if any of it was real.

What purpose and meaning are there if nothing is real? If the laughter and love were made with a diagnosed narcissist who may have felt no love or joy, did it really happen? Like the tree that falls in the forest when no one is around. Did it make a sound?

For me I have felt grief as a physical pain in my chest. Heavy. Sometimes, I feel frozen in place. And sometimes it's a boulder in my throat, closing it down, making it hard to breathe and I can't find my voice. Other times, I want to scream or run. Sometimes there is nowhere to put the grief. And the pain becomes physical manifestations.

REPENTANCE AND REPAIR

Rabbi Danya Ruttenberg (2022) explains that it takes five stages for repentance and repair to occur through action, not words:

- Stage One is the confession, where the person owns what they have done and accepts accountability for any harm they have caused.
- In Stage Two, they start to change. The person commits to the process to learn and grow to make different choices. This may be done in various ways, for example, through therapy or a mentor.
- Stage Three is where they make amends. The person takes real action to make amends.
- Stage Four (only after Stages One to Three are

complete) is when the person makes an apology for the harm they have caused and their actions.
- Stage Five occurs when the person chooses to behave in a different way the next time the same situation appears to harm anyone.

Sadly for my children, myself, and many victim-survivors, accountability, repentance, and repair are something we never get to experience. We find a way to find acceptance and heal while also never fully having all the answers and never having had closure or witnessing remorse or an apology.

I supported my abuser emotionally and financially through the process of separation. I had found out about years of deceit and was coming to terms with the realisation of what he had put me through and the consequences of his actions for all of us. Yet, I wanted our friends to care for him, and I wanted to save face for us as a family. He was, of course, also my children's father, and I was still hoping for as amicable as possible divorce. He saw that as an opportunity. He turned the whole story around. He vilified me and continued to financially and emotionally abuse me, refusing me information and access. He isolated me from my friends, told people I deserted him in his time of need, made accusations that I was "alienating" his children, and played the victim well.

I arranged accommodation and paid his rent, gave him money, and got a car for him. He abandoned the car I had given him in a laneway, with the registration needing to be renewed, and posted the keys to me. The car accumulated fines for not being registered and being there too long. The car was taken away from me as it had been loaned to me by a charity. The charity was incredibly angry that the precious resource had been treated like that. (This was classic narcissistic, manipulative behaviour to try to ruin my relationship and credibility and lose the car, causing me stress and costing me money.)

He played mind games, calling me, frantic that he had run out of money for food. Although I was still supporting him financially a year later, I found out he had been working during this time, receiving insurance payouts and government subsidies. I stopped paying his rent and bills.

During my post-separation abuse, my ex kept trying to provoke a response from me, using various tactics, including:

- He sent a constant stream of emails, calls, and texts from himself and then from his lawyers, all demanding, intimidating, manipulative, threatening, and abusive.
- He constantly monitored our social media and watched where we were through common friends or institutions (stalking).
- He applied for an intervention order against my father, perjuring himself under oath multiple times.
- He gave false information to government organisations (Centrelink and Child Support), hiding bank accounts and creating huge amounts of costs through adjournments and cross-applications.
- He defied intervention orders just enough to be intimidating but not enough for police to be able to take it to court.
- He looked at me like he was going to kill me—a look many other survivors have described to me. A look that made me physically sick and brought on panic

attacks.

Each week, for seven years, there would be another fire to put out. His behaviour was premeditated, well-thought-out, and included a series of decisions made for maximum impact and destruction. Court dates, police visits, and letters were all chosen to collide with major occasions, birthdays, exams, musicals, or graduations. More stress, more anxiety, more money, more exhaustion.

I had more skills to learn. More incredible people to meet. A community to surround us with support. More strength to find within myself. More safety and love to focus on my children. More resolve to fight on and get to the end. More mistakes to make and lessons to learn. More peace to find within as the cyclone built around.

I learned to accept that I will never get an apology. Will never get those years back. Will never get the promised or imagined future. And began to let it be. I know without doubt there were moments of pure happiness that I experienced that no one could take away from me, whether they were genuine or not, for me they were real. I loved with all my heart and gave with every part of myself. I did my best. I felt joy. I smiled and danced and sang. It was real for me. I did have happiness. And the future is in my hands, and it will be full of the meaning and joy I create.

We get to choose. Living with a closed heart or open heart. Living full of bitterness or kindness. A life of hatred or compassion. We may have wounds and nightmares and grief, but we can still choose growth and meaning and fighting for justice.

We may never get the remedy we deserve, no apology or

accountability or time recovered, or answers or youth returned. We may see no regret or remorse from our abuser or the system that aided them.

We can connect with a new tribe, make a difference in just one person's life, and we can create safe places to tell our stories and listen and acknowledge others.

LESSONS I HAVE LEARNED:

- We can choose to live with an open heart.
- We can thrive not just survive.
- We can write our ending differently.

TEN

The Stolen Farthings

DISHONESTY AND DISHARMONY

Economic abuse is a lifelong barrier to safety.
—T. Casselson

Not only had he not prepared me for the avalanche headed my way and had kept me completely in the dark throughout our marriage, but he also went on to blame me for the collapse. It was all my fault!

While I was in shock and trying to piece the puzzle together, he proclaimed I was a spender and not an earner: my health expenses, elaborate parties, school expenses… (classic DARVO).

He didn't tell anyone my income had steadily increased since we had arrived in Australia. I had been working the same job all along. He didn't tell anyone I had never had access to more than a little pocket money that he controlled. When I organised parties, they were based on a budget from him, and all final decisions were made by him.

Everything was controlled by him. I didn't buy groceries without him. Millions of dollars of debt built up by him was blamed on me. The general rule about narcissists is that whatever they are accusing, they are confessing. When I look back at years of accusations my ex made at people, each one was a confession of his own behaviour.

While people use the terms "economic" and "financial" abuse interchangeably, financial abuse is a subset of economic abuse. The Centre for Women's Economic Safety defines economic abuse as "including financial abuse and a form of family violence in which one person controls, exploits, or sabotages another person's economic resources (e.g. money, property, transport, employment), limiting their autonomy and threatening their economic security and wellbeing" (*CWES— Centre for Women's Economic Safety*, n.d.).

- Control/Restrict—limit ability to access of resources, e.g. giving you a small allowance and restricting access to bank accounts.
- Exploit—misuse resources, e.g. gambling, signing debt in your name.
- Sabotage—limit potential options, e.g. stop you from working or studying (*CWES—Centre for Women's Economic Safety*, n.d.).

Economic abuse allows the abuser to have complete control over the family member or partner, keep them in the relationship, and stop them from achieving safety if they leave the relationship (WIRE, 2018).

Abusers often use the excuse of "being helpful" as a way of not allowing information to get to the family members or their partner.

My ex told people I was unwell and he was protecting me, which was why they shouldn't tell me he was borrowing money from them.

This means the abuser has even more power and more control. The abuser has more access to information and confidence.

This cumulative effect results in abusers holding more power during and even after the relationship.

The result is that the victim-survivor doesn't have a true picture of the financial circumstances (often for many years) and has reduced financial literacy and confidence. It means starting and rebuilding from a calamitous state.

In my situation (as in many others), my ex "looked after" the finances and admin tasks by taking it "off my shoulders" and not "wanting any added pressure" for me. He begged people not to tell me about money he had borrowed to "take care of" me and my "needs." He gained more control and more power over me. He built up more debt over more years and became more confident with the greater power and control he had, and I had no idea it was happening.

It is difficult to explain the full impact of financial abuse. To be lied to and cheated on by the person I trusted the most. For this person to have been stealing from me for years and smiling while they did it. For this person to borrow a million dollars of debt, put it in my name, and not take any responsibility. To take out triple mortgages without my knowledge. For this person to sign legal documents stating that I was aware of all transactions and had been given legal advice on all decisions. For this person to borrow money from our closest friends and family, using me as an excuse for some of these transactions, asking some not to tell me, and expecting others would not. For this person to deny me access to the money I earned. For this person to steal all the money my children had saved. That I believed I had saved.

It is difficult to explain how this feels, the shattering of one's essence, one's very being. Like you are worthless. Like you are a fool. Like nothing you have known or know is true.

Then there was the humiliation, shock, and shame when this person then blamed me for this huge amount of debt. The feeling of overwhelm. Or when some people doubted that I could not have known about the huge accumulating debt. I lost trust in myself and my judgement. I felt a total ignoramus. I felt grief for a life that did not exist. A bond that never existed. An imagined partnership, trust, and love that was never there.

And then there were people who minimised the impact. Even after looking at the evidence and web of lies and shock I was in, some people minimised the deceit, and many made excuses for the behaviour. In a way, they were invested in protecting themselves and denying they had been a victim also.

IDENTIFYING FEATURES

A clue, on reflection, was a lack of compassion. The abuser understands what people are going through and can use that knowledge to manipulate them but can't seem to feel any care towards people. They have a heightened sense of importance and get easily wounded if you don't admire them.

The first time my ex picked me up to take me on a date, my mother told him to drive carefully because he had precious property. He said, "We are all precious." Of course, we all laughed. On its own, it's a funny throwaway line. When you look at an accumulation of these comments, you see someone entitled with feelings of grandiosity.

An abuser will do anything to get what they want. They don't care who or what they destroy. My ex told people he was going to "make her so sick that she will be in hospital constantly" (in discussions about me) during my seven years of post-separation abuse. Abusers will do anything to punish and exhaust the healthy parent. They're totally self-involved, with no care for the children or interest in the impact on them.

The day after his first suicide attempt, I found him trying

to borrow money, and then six years post discovery of his deceit, he was still borrowing money, still hiding money, still manipulating people. He still had not declared himself insolvent. He was driven to achieve his means no matter the consequences and nothing was more important.

LESSONS I HAVE LEARNED:

- Financial abuse is devastating. Don't underestimate the damage to the victim.
- It is difficult to know who is vulnerable:
  - Lack of self-identifying—We do not see ourselves as being in a financial abuse situation until a lot of damage is done.
  - Misguided assumptions—Systems, banks, people, and organisations around us make incorrect assumptions about both the victim and the perpetrator that allows the perpetrator to misuse and abuse the system and the victim.
- The key is to look for accumulated behaviour:
  - Controlled behaviour.
  - The ability to maintain a façade.
  - The insistence on secrecy.
  - Private meetings.
  - Isolating the victim.
  - Making comments to discredit the victim's mental or physical state.

ELEVEN

The Emperor's New Clothing

GRIMM TRAGEDY AND PROTOCOLS

> *People see what they choose to see,*
> *even in the face of evidence to the contrary.*
> —T. Casselson

We too have the power to choose. To change our minds. We can leave a situation. We can choose to be healthy and not live in a toxic relationship or toxic environment. We have the strength to choose our children and ourselves. We have the strength to choose bravery over fear. We can find the courage to trust ourselves and leave. (It has to be the right time and circumstances for us.)

Sadly, there is still a lot of shame and stigma around emotional issues in our society. A discomfort with suffering that leads to a push towards rushing our healing process. We want everybody to be fine, to get over their pain and grief and trauma. To let it go, move on. Don't bear a grudge. Be positive. Forgive. People are uncomfortable when we suffer or are in pain, so they want us to "get over it." Some people also become uncomfortable with any positive progress we make for ourselves and prefer that we stay the way we were before because they know how to deal with "that" person.

And enabling my ex's behaviour did not help him. It also hurt my children.

By not challenging him, some family and friends perpetuated his story. By writing a letter stating that he had attended therapy sessions in Sydney, he was able to bypass face-to-face therapy recommended here in Melbourne and not take a men's behaviour change course seriously, making jokes about me and the participants. His 'friends' enabled him to not pay child support by giving him cash for jobs and encouraged this behaviour. And the friend who gave the location of me and my children to the ex I was petrified of, even when I had asked them not to.

Instead of protecting the victims of intimidation, certain people used pressure and guilt on my teenagers to see their father when he was being abusive, threatening, and toxic.

Often the enablers do not mean harm; one enabler pressured me to give a car I had been given from a charity to my perpetrator without understanding the consequences and then, when he was supposed to be safeguarding money, gave half of it to the perpetrator without discussing it with me.

And while I was caught up in shock, shame, disillusion, incomprehension, guilt, disbelief, and so much grief, the thing that struck me was how much over-explaining I was doing. I was still trying to work it out myself so I couldn't form clear sentences, and yet I wanted and needed support. I have always been THE supporter, but when the time came for troops to gather, a void appeared. There were some tremendous people who helped with practical things—gathered to pack up our house in an emergency or offered a car for us to drive—but people did not want to hear us or acknowledge what was happening on an emotional level.

Some of the closest people in my life did not want to hear that I had been betrayed in every way possible by this man I had trusted my entire adult life. Not only did they not want to hear, but they chose to make excuses for his behaviour and support him rather than support me and our children. As horrific as it sounds, I wondered how different things would have been if my ex had died. That type of loss is acknowledged; is understood, is comprehensible to people, ours was ignored.

I had witnessed my childhood sweetheart almost lose his life. My children were suddenly dealing with that as well, with no warning, losing everything material, all security.

Why do "good people" think that doing nothing and saying nothing is good enough?

So many of the "do-gooders" told me, "In the interest of… you should…" Some shared their opinions with my young children, that they thought my children should spend time with their father, who continued to refuse to financially support them. He also continued to harass, taunt, and mistreat them. These same people didn't feel their own children were old enough to hear what we were going through but were happy to advise my traumatised children to get over it and support their father.

Court-appointed officials, psychologists, and psychiatrists were saying something else. These officials all agreed that the children should not see their father until he got some help. My job as a mother was to keep my children safe.

When I was fighting for my gett and being emotionally and verbally abused, the Chief Rabbi was being verbally abused by my abuser, too. His lawyer was sending threatening emails and demanding apologies. I was in and out of court. These same "good people" stood by and refused to say anything. Not one of these "good" people sat my ex down to discuss gett refusal or respect. A "close" friend asked me, "Why is it important to you?" Instead of questioning my abuser for withholding the religious divorce, the question was put to me as to why I was pushing for it. They all wanted it to go away. No one wanted the fuss.

I was told I was alienating people. My family. My friends.

I was asked why I wanted to be isolated.

My ex was kept protected by the Shule (a Jewish place of worship) community as a member.

My children did not get calls to check if they were OK.

I was not isolating myself or alienating anyone. I was setting boundaries. For the first time ever.

It is beyond comprehension that "do-gooders" feel they can step in and tell children how to behave towards a person they have been abused by and that the court system has declared dangerous for them to be around. It is dumbfounding how those "upstanding citizens" who knew that the abuser had lied, cheated, and betrayed his family could protect and entertain the abuser over the said family. For people to use their value system as a reason they can't break ties with an abuser is downright confusing. Triggering.

It is difficult to understand why friends, family, or care workers may minimise the seriousness of emotional abuse. "Well, at least it wasn't physical or sexual abuse." "We only saw him being a good father." "You were always so happy." Some questioned me with cynicism, and some were afraid to question their judgement as to whether my assessment was correct. Some could not deal with the cognitive dissonance (when we feel discomfort that our behaviour doesn't align with our beliefs or two beliefs don't align). Others felt I might be blaming them. None of this was true. I was just trying to make sense of my world.

And the excuses kept coming:

- "The pressures of life are overwhelming."
- "It happened to my sister, and she found the strength

to forgive him and take him back."
- "Men try to hold the burden alone and don't know how to talk."

Why is it that so many people feel the need to make excuses for a man who has been cheating, lying, committing fraud, and betraying his wife, friends, and the law for years and years? People downplayed his actions, excused his behaviour, and minimised the fact that financial abuse is intimate terrorism with incredible consequences. That it leads to devastating consequences: homelessness, incredible debt, low self-esteem, and anxiety, just to name a few.

So often, perpetrators frame isolation tactics, financial mismanagement, and deceit as them "taking care of their partner," borrowing the money to "look after" the partner, and not wanting to "cause anxiety or stress" for the partner. Control of the narrative is the motive; the perpetrator accompanies you to each doctor's visit as a "caring" gesture, often speaking for you when asked questions. Control and manipulation. Ensuring you stick to the script. Let me be clear—any one of these things could be seen as being a caring, concerned, and loving partner. That is why coercive control is so difficult to spot and so difficult to identify, even for the victim. There are good moments. Misery and degradation are interspersed with gifts, praise, and loving gestures. Reward and punishment hold you in place. Confuses you. It makes you feel like you might be causing the outburst or imagining the cruelty and fear-inducing behaviour.

Perpetrators set it up to take the children to sports so as to be seen as being involved and contributing while you are set up doing chores at home. They will cook the highlight of the meal while you cook all the side dishes, and they will tell people they do the cooking. It sounds almost inconceivable, but they will send you grocery shopping and want to be responsible for shopping for the highlight of the meal themselves and then tell people they do the shopping and cooking. The narrative becomes very clear: how much they do around the home. They weaponise your health conditions to make themselves look like the long suffering partner. Again, they play the hero caregiver in the story.

LESSONS I HAVE LEARNED:

- When the victim-survivor feels unheard or unseen, there are consequences.
- Not acknowledging the victim-survivor can lead to:
    - Triggering the victim-survivor, which can lead them to an immediate or delayed reaction. They may become disoriented, disconnected, sad, confused, or anxious, or they may have nightmares later.
    - Re-traumatising the victim-survivor.
    - Re-victimising the victim-survivor.
    - Labelling the victim-survivor.
    - Making the victim-survivor feel blamed, shamed, discounted, or isolated.
    - Gaslighting the victim-survivor.
    - Sending victims back to their abusers.

TWELVE

Goldilocks

RESPONSIBILITY FOR OUR ACTIONS

> *We must let go of the life we have planned*
> *so as to accept the one that is waiting for us.*
> —Joseph Campbell

There is a difference between sitting in traffic and accepting your situation with grace, putting on a podcast or music, and being calm versus being joyful, grateful, and happy about the situation. Toxic positivity is denying your emotions and allowing them to fester inside you. They escape as physical or psychological symptoms or bigger illnesses later.

If we want true healing and happiness, we need to recognise each emotion, acknowledge it, feel it, and let it pass through us. True resilience is not "having no emotion"; it is being able to have emotions, knowing they will pass and that you will be OK. It's holding onto hope for a better day.

Survivors often share common characteristics: empathy, caring nature, kindness, compassion, cooperation, and patience. I do not share this to make you want to close yourself off, rather to make you lean in to people who are kind and compassionate too. Don't settle for less. Be open and trusting with a select few.

I love the incredibly powerful metaphor of building an island by Glennon Doyle (2020). She talks about building an island with a moat around it and a drawbridge. Anyone can visit her on her island if they are prepared to accept her as she is. She says it is not her duty to convince everyone to accept and respect her and her children. It is her duty to allow onto her island only those who already respect and accept her and her children. Only those people who will walk across the drawbridge as "beloved, respectful guests they are" are allowed access to her island.

The day I decided to escape my abuser, I lifted the drawbridge and began to set up boundaries to keep myself and my children safe. Slowly, I have strengthened those boundaries. People can visit my island if they respect and accept me and my children: what we stand for and what keeps our island a safe place.

My island is a place of love, kindness, care, compassion, inclusion, respect, and one without fear. It doesn't matter who a person is; they can't visit if they bring fear, disrespect or unkindness. It's not me alienating myself or my children; it's me protecting and being a role model for boundaries and self-respect. (Of course, this is easier said than done, so I am a constant work in progress.)

We need to disengage from people who don't support and believe us. It means if people are going to give unsolicited advice, even if they feel they are doing the right thing, they are uninvited. We surround ourselves with people who champion us, encourage us, believe in us, and love us. By this I do not mean 'yes' people. I love people who challenge me. Their purpose needs to be to see me win, they need to believe me and believe in me.

You learn very quickly, as difficult as it is, to set boundaries. It is even more onerous to keep those boundaries in place. People do not like boundaries. They will challenge the boundary and you. They will try to provoke you. They will do this consciously and sometimes unconsciously. If you understand why you set up your moat and built that drawbridge, you will be able to be firm with the boundary, protecting yourself and your children.

Transparency and boundaries do not mean you do not

trust the other person; it ensures you have trust and ensures you share the burden and responsibility. Transparency and boundaries are the foundation of healthy communication and create deeper emotional connections. Transparency differs from honesty in that you proactively share information. You make sure everything is on the table. This means avoiding miscommunication, conflict, and misunderstandings.

YELLOW ROCK COMMUNICATION

There is great confusion and stress when trying to communicate with a narcissist. This occurs in all forms of communication: face-to-face, telephone, email, and text. There is no congruence, consistency, or clarity. Everything can be twisted and misinterpreted and turned against you.

Over these many years, I have experimented with grey rock communication—leaving all emotions out of communication—only facts, only essentials. This is not the best solution, as the narcissist can take offence. People around the narcissist (flying monkeys and court officials) may also get offended on behalf of the abuser.

A better option is yellow rock communication (Swithin, n.d.). If you have to communicate, add niceties and be courteous as if always imagining you are being overheard by a court official. Choosing to respond and not react. Narcissists are known to try to bait their victims to react with comments or glares. Don't allow them to derail you. When we react, they use it against us and say we are "crazy," "overreacting," and "unhinged."

Have standard responses prepared. Stay focused on the

task at hand. If you need to, take a breath or walk away to recenter yourself. Try repeating your name to yourself three times. You will feel re-embodied.

LESSONS I HAVE LEARNED:

- For a person to survive and thrive, they need to feel safe and empowered.
- Support includes offering:
  - Immediate safe housing and financial aid.
  - Comfort, compassion, and kindness.
  - Skills training in feeling empowered, financial management, assertive language, and legal aid, (depending on the persons needs).
  - Safe places to share stories and connect.
  - Trauma-informed counselling and alternative healing modalities.
- Limit communication with an abuser. If you have to communicate because of shared children, try yellow rock communication.
  - Stay on the issue
  - Be polite (imagine court officials are listening always).
- Implementing firm boundaries can affirm your rights and increase emotional safety.

THIRTEEN

Snow White

KINDNESS MATTERS

Bread for all, and roses too.
—Helen Todd

Kindness, connection, and compassion are a balm to healing.
Soul-soothing, heart-healing,
huggers, listeners,
they witness our stories,
hold us during our breakdowns and celebrate us through our breakthroughs—
these are our people.

The actual healing, the decision to heal, the work, has to be done by each individual. It took me time in therapy and alternative healing to let go of that sense of duty and responsibility to "fix" another. No one can save anyone else.

I am responsible for my safety and happiness. I am responsible to keep my children safe. We all need to take responsibility for our own healing. We all need to take responsibility for our own happiness. We can hold space for each other. We can offer compassion and love to each other, but we cannot fix each other—as much as we wish we could.

As for those "good people" who chose to abandon us, what a lost opportunity for them to be a role model for their children in how to show kindness. How to show being empowered. There is an incredible grief in realising this. It is painful to experience the loss of those you thought were close friends, who, in fact, revealed themselves as only "fair-weather" friends.

On the other hand, we mustn't put unrealistic expectations on others. We hope our friends will support us, but we never know which way they will go until they are challenged.

How lucky I was that other beautiful, strong women and men stood up with me. How lucky for me that all along my journey, as these so called "good people" have fallen away, many more incredible, brave women and men who have voices and wisdom have stood beside me and mentored me, have seen me, listened to me, guided me, helped me find my voice, helped me discover (and rediscover) and hold firm my boundaries, helped me heal and heal again.

These people have listened to me. They have believed in me and my children and championed me. They have spoken up for me not only when I was beside them but when I wasn't. They believed I deserved more, and they helped me believe in myself.

There are those few special, intuitive people who really did and continue to see me. Those who remind me that I matter. Those who acknowledge my pain. Those who look me in the eyes. Those who make me feel I am sane and that my reality is visible. There are a few who were able to see through the smoke and mirrors of the magnetic charm of the narcissistic traits and admit that they noticed he was cold to me, that he was unkind to me when he thought no one was looking. Some had an instant dislike for him that they couldn't explain. People who picked up on whispers, on red flags.

To me, people seemed uneasy and unsure how to behave after the first suicide attempt happened. So many traumas packed together: attempted suicide, homelessness, financial crisis, divorce, intervention orders. No one wants to talk. No one knows what to say or do or how to help.

Police, lawyers and courts involved. If people didn't want to be actively caught up before, they definitely disappeared as things escalated.

No one wanted to hear or acknowledge in case they had to have an opinion or take sides. No one wants to be touched by the curse.

My initial feeling was shame. And a need to keep in control. Keep it together, keep going. And then the adrenaline kicked in and it was pure warrior. I was the fierce protector. Always ready in survival mode.

Connecting with other victim-survivors gave me an incredible community of people who spoke a similar language of pain and grief and hope for the future.

Each one of us can play a part in ending intimate partner abuse. It begins with educating ourselves and ensuring we are not enabling the perpetrators. We need to assess our forms of communication and procedures and policies. We can be patient and explain decisions being made—educate people. Each of us holds a key to the solution. Knowledge is power.

KEY LESSONS I HAVE LEARNED:

- Safety and support of victims is essential.
- Throughout this book, we have mentioned what not to say to trauma survivors. We know it is easy to get it wrong unintentionally. Most people are doing their best. However, here is a cheat sheet to guide you:
- What NOT to say:
    - We didn't see it.
    - You are overreacting.
    - I know how you feel.
    - We have to walk on eggshells around you.
    - Move on.
    - Let go.
    - Forgive.
    - Don't hold a grudge.
    - We have to stay neutral.
    - There are two sides to every story.
- Words of affirmation, acknowledgement and connection include:
    - I hear you.
    - I believe you.
    - I've got you.
    - What do you need?
    - I'm listening.
    - Can I sit with you?
    - How can I support you?

FOURTEEN

The Little Match Girl

DOING NOTHING DOES NOTHING

> *It is not the critic who counts; not the man who points out how the strong man stumbles, or where the doer of deeds could have done them better. The credit belongs to the man who is actually in the arena, whose face is marred by dust and sweat and blood; who strives valiantly; who errs, who comes short again and again, because there is no effort without error and shortcoming; but who does actually strive to do the deeds; who knows great enthusiasms, the great devotions; who spends himself in a worthy cause; who at the best knows in the end the triumph of high achievement, and who at the worst, if he fails, at least fails while daring greatly, so that his place shall never be with those cold and timid souls who neither know victory nor defeat.*
>
> —Theodore Roosevelt

Part of the problem with coercive control and post-separation abuse is that we try to work within a broken system that enables systems abuse, false allegations, and years of ongoing pain, stress, and economic destruction. Some police officers who don't understand threatening behaviour say, "Come back when he does what he has threatened" or "It's not family violence if you are not a family." Police can't do anything, even with an intervention order, even if they want to, or even if they are frustrated, until there are multiple offences with evidence. Stalking without photographs to prove it is not stalking.

There is great stress in this huge, broken system where you are fighting to keep your children safe, and you feel completely disempowered. Too many moments to record. Triggering moments, utter panic, fear, and exhaustion. On one of these occasions, I sat in a designated safe room as my daughter was interviewed by a court-appointed official (court reporter) who would write a report and also decide, on the spot, whether to allow our abuser access for a meeting with my terrified daughter. I was physically ill with anxiety at not being able to protect my child. I had been grilled by this same court reporter just a short time earlier. She had been particularly nasty in her approach. She had attempted to provoke me a number of times. I asked her why she was doing that. She told me that was how she worked—that she would question me and my ex in the same way. From this, she would decide what the truth was, and she would then make decisions and report her findings. My child's safety sat in this cold woman's hands. I cried. I stuttered. I was not very clear in my statement. My answers were not smooth or well-spoken. I cried some more. I told her that my abuser would come across as charismatic. I told her that he would be much better at this than me. He was a salesman. He could sell anything. People loved him. He WAS a smooth talker. Words rolled off his tongue. I cried some more. She showed no emotion. She just told me this was only about me. And my relationship with my daughter. That my ex was not relevant to our discussion. She wanted to know if I had coached my daughter. It seemed like she had already decided I had. She told me she was a professional. Somehow, that didn't make me feel better, it did not inspire any confidence in the process.

And so I sat for what felt like forever. Crying, feeling like I couldn't breathe, feeling nauseous, feeling helpless. Across from me, not one but two women sat crying, as both had their parenting orders handed down that day. Both were physical and emotional abuse survivors. Both had been told they had to hand over their young children (one an infant) to their abusers for unsupervised visitations. Why would a judge think a man who abused could be trusted to not abuse her child? One woman who had been punched in the stomach during pregnancy now sat sobbing in the corner. She had been ordered to give her child over to the man who punched her unborn child.

The court reporter's approach did provoke my abuser. He didn't like to be spoken to with disrespect. He showed himself. She refused to allow him access to my daughter. He really showed his true colours and and began his entitled performance. My daughter, my father, and I were ushered out to a safe exit by a security officer. Down the passage, we could hear my abuser's behaviour escalating. My daughter would not be forced to see him. I could catch my breath. Today I had kept my child safe.

There is no neutral position in an abusive situation. A survivor of abuse needs to feel safe. A relationship where people choose to remain neutral is not a safe relationship to be in. A survivor of abuse needs to be given agency, heard, seen, and acknowledged. If you cannot offer this, you are not a safe place and you are not helping the survivor heal. You would be an unsafe space, re-traumatising and triggering to the survivor. You are, in fact, discounting their experiences and making them feel more isolated and alone. I was dumbfounded when I explained to certain friends how afraid I was of my abuser and they minimised or ignored my fears. It completely discounted my reality. For me feeling unsafe triggers my body. Feeling unsafe can come from internal and external changes including certain thoughts, memories, body sensations, sounds, smells, stress, feeling too hot.

PANIC ATTACK

Pain in my chest. Heart palpitations. Tears flooding my eyes.

Headache increasing in intensity. Panic building.

Self-talk. "Breathe." "I am OK. I am OK. I am OK."

Breathing in slowly, breathing out.

"Slow down."

I am seven years out of my abusive relationship, and yet a trigger can still send my nervous system into panic.

Fight, flight, freeze.

I was sitting in a bank manager's office, on my own, withdrawing money out of an assurance account set up as a bank guarantee for my parents' immigration to Australia. First, my identity had been flagged as someone had been trying to get details of my account. Flutters began in my tummy when this was disclosed. Secondly, as my details were brought up on the screen, three accounts popped up.

All my debt had been wiped at this and other financial institutions due to financial abuse six years ago. Three accounts should not have appeared. Symptoms began: mind fog, nausea, headache, sweaty palms. Calm as I could, I asked what the accounts were. Apparently, a debt of $45,000. TRIGGER. The neurons in my brain started firing wildly. Questions raced: Was this all happening again? Had he amassed new debt in my name? Was it just this bank, or was there more?

After much discussion and offers of water and apologies, there was more discussion. The young lady helping me needed to get assistance from senior staff members.

More discussions. More tears from me. I was having an

out-of-body experience.

With apologies, they explained that it was his debt. I was just a cardholder. I asked to be removed from the account. I asked if they could please speed things up. I needed to leave. They looked flustered.

The money would be released. They would not charge admin fees for the transaction.

I walked out shaking.

A few seconds later, I was breathing. I was OK.

This is me, healed and healing. I am recovering from post-traumatic stress disorder (PTSD). The worst of my symptoms include:

- Frequent nightmares where I wake my daughter with my screams.
- Flashbacks at inconvenient times, a sudden reliving of a terrible event or moment.
- Anxiety at times, including experiencing a number of panic attacks.
- Isolating myself.
- Times when it is incredibly difficult to concentrate.
- Often, when I am on edge or hypervigilant, I'm always on the lookout for triggers and highly reactive to seemingly neutral stimuli like a loud sound or a bright light. I burst into tears at a small upset or jump at a minor disruption.

I realised I had put off going into the bank to carry out this simple task for over a month, as anything that could trigger me raises my stress levels and begins to make me feel panicked. This delay was completely on an unconscious level until I started to reflect on the day. As I write this now, my breath moves from my diaphragm to my chest. I feel like a weight is sitting there; it starts to close tightly, and an uncomfortable pain starts to rise in the centre. The pain will increase in intensity if I don't take control of my breathing. I know to you, the reader, it may sound like I am overreacting. My calm mind judges me harshly. My body, however, is triggered. A loud noise, someone yelling, an associated smell, certain places or people. That is what post-traumatic stress is.

My ex refused to pay child support, hid income with the help of "do-gooder" friends, did jobs for cash, received money from Centrelink, and received income protection. He played the system and played me. He swore he loved his children but went on holidays overseas and flaunted going out to expensive restaurants.

At first, I was too in fear for our lives to even attempt to get child support. Later, he evaded and fought any attempt at child support.

He drained every cent I had. He dragged out the court proceedings as long and as far as he could. I tried being my own advocate, but the judge did not like it. In the intervention court case, I represented myself twice, and the stress was excruciating. Judges do not like you to self-represent. (Although, it can be done.) My abuser's lawyers were aggressive and nasty and very difficult to work with. More systems abuse. Thousands of wasted dollars. More financial abuse.

There are further far-reaching consequences: loss of security I had been building for years, being homeless, having to accept food parcels at one time, living in social housing, not taking holidays, destruction of credit ratings, loss of a foundation, and more humiliation and shame.

LESSONS I HAVE LEARNED:

- One of the biggest healing mechanisms is our breath, learning to come home to ourselves.
- We can regulate our nervous system through breathwork. Breath is medicine.
- Try this simple breath-grounding exercise:
- Put your hand over the centre of your chest.
  - Breathe in slowly through your nose, hold, and breathe out slowly through your mouth.
  - Repeat three times.
  - If it is comfortable to do so, close your eyes while you do this.
  - Repeat throughout the day.

FIFTEEN

The Three Little Pigs

FOUNDATIONS OF STRENGTH

Grief and resilience live together.
—Michelle Obama

Seven years after everything blew up on ground zero day, on a particularly ordinary afternoon, I was informed my childhood-sweetheart-turned-nightmare-abuser had died by suicide. A deep sadness broke in me. I was shattered by the end of any hope of healing for him, any hope of reconnecting for my children, any return of the handsome, funny, charming man I had known for a brief moment and had given my entire heart to for most of my life.

Unlike with escaping family violence, death brought protocols which I was grateful for. My family and friends wrapped their arms around me. There was a constant supply of delicious comfort foods: bagels, smoked salmon, cakes, quiche, and chocolate (protocol one—feed the mourners). There was an outpouring of text messages and phone calls of support and love from around the world (protocol two—offer sympathy). A constant flow of visitors dropped by (protocol three—do not leave the mourners alone). There was an incredible depth of care, compassion, and kindness that surrounded us, literally holding us in our grief (very complicated grief).

We followed step-by-step procedures for mourning, grieving, praying, and sitting. So many gathered and reached out, wanting to hear and acknowledge, giving us permission to lean into our grief.

A couple of flying monkeys warned me not to attend the funeral. One went as far as threatening me. There were hateful glares and snubs at my children from people who had been so close to us and knew my children well. We have endured so much that a few snubs, glares, and warnings bounce off us. They say much more about the people doing the hating than the people grieving and standing tall.

I could not have been prouder of my children being respectful, standing united and walking holding hands behind their fathers coffin as it was taken for burial. As they had done their entire lives they rose up and held each other with calm and courage.

According to the latest report by the Coroner's Court of Victoria (2024) provides details for all deaths by suicide, one in three people had been exposed to family violence. (Experience of Family Violence, 2024)

- In 28.2% of the cases family violence had been present in the history of the case.
- In half of these the person who died by suicide was the perpetrator of violence.
- This was a gendered difference with significantly more males (65%) than females (16%) recorded as the violence perpetrator.
- More research needs to be done and this report does not go into causation. It does highlight mental health as an issue, with nearly three quarters of those with a history of family violence as having been diagnosed with a mental illness.
- Legal stressors were present in over 60% of male family perpetrators who died by suicide.

Support

We were surrounded by love. We had a community who cared and loved and supported us. And that is what we focused on.

We are survivors.

We really do need a protocol for victim-survivors of domestic violence like there is for death. Trauma is a form of grief, and we need people to hold us, acknowledge us, and wrap us in the same blanket of care, compassion, and comfort.

Healing is not a straight line when life has been controlled and manipulated by one person and that person tries to strip you of everything (or you have suffered from some other form of trauma): all possessions, the roof over your head, decision-making power, safety, your history that you thought was true, the essence of you, including your self-esteem.

Healing is messy. It's made up of good days and bad days. One moment, you'll feel free and strong, like the survivor warrior you are, and the next moment, you'll be triggered and crawl into the foetal position, hand on heart, self-soothing.

The good news is the transition to good moments seems to get smoother and quicker as you learn more skills and tools to deal with those difficult moments.

Abuse survivors carry a huge amount of shame, especially around feeling stupid and being taken advantage of. You feel like you can't trust your judgement, so how can you trust others?

I felt so stupid to have lived with this man who had deceived me for so many years and not suspected anything.

That this man had total control of everything—how had that even happened? That he had manipulated and charmed and fooled many people while I was right there. He had borrowed from friends, family, banks, institutions, and dangerous loan sharks. So many questions, so much shock.

I was full of shame and sadness and sorrow and pain and horror and then fear and later anger. I am still working on acceptance and meaning. We jump back between different emotions—again, there are no straight lines.

I wanted so badly for my abuser to show remorse. I had to accept he never would.

Healing is a forever journey. It begins with acceptance of where you are at. For me, the first step was pure adrenaline-pumping survival—getting through every day literally by the minute. I had to break up the huge number of tasks that had to be done into achievable chunks. And, I had to just keep moving. Even slow movement. Forward movement.

As long as I had some forward momentum, I was able to deal with the emotional wreckage. My children and I had emotional support from the day after the first suicide attempt. It is incredibly important for resources to be available and people around to provide emotional refuge and safety. We were incredibly lucky to have the knowledge of and access to a social worker, a general practitioner, and a psychologist who could provide us with comfort, validation, and acknowledgement of our pain and grief. (See the Resources chapter and reach out for support).

The good news is that we can begin again and rewrite our story. It is never too late. We can choose who we want to be, with intention and with purpose—one small step at a time.

One of the biggest steps in healing is learning that what other people think of you is none of your business. Growing up in a community that focuses on "What will people think?" as a key ingredient to behaviour was a huge burden to let go of. A huge weight to put down. It continues to be an ongoing project. Some days are easier than others, and I can get caught out sometimes when unhelpful comments come my way. The important thing to remember is that it is a work in progress.

Learning to trust our own judgement again, knowing that our intuition is incredibly strong, and leaning into our intuition takes time and self-compassion. Loving and trusting oneself takes courage.

Self-compassion teaches us to be kind to ourselves. We can be so kind to others, so compassionate, and yet so hard on ourselves. Learning to not judge ourselves too harshly when we make mistakes, learning to speak with kindness to ourselves, and giving ourselves permission to self-nurture can be particularly difficult when you have been a victim of gaslighting from an abusive partner whose sole purpose was to undermine you. Learn to self-soothe. Learn to say no. Love can heal us, and the best place to begin is to learn self-love. Some days, you may feel unlovable, and it can be helpful to recognise that as a "leftover" from the campaign your abuser was raging against you all these years. It doesn't mean other people see you that way.

Many people find this confronting and difficult—to nurture oneself and care for oneself and to talk kindly to oneself. What would you say if you were talking to a close friend in need? Nurture yourself through discovering your strengths and focusing on what you do well. Nurture yourself with rest. We find it very difficult to give ourselves permission to rest and recharge.

Trusting others takes a leap of faith. Have belief in yourself and use that intuition. It takes time, patience, and practice. Without trust, there cannot be connection. It may be hard to trust again, so acknowledge that reality and go gently. To live a life of joy, we need to live with an open heart and let people in. We can choose to live open-heartedly and open-mindedly and live full and happy lives. To be coffee beans.

One of the most difficult parts of healing is protecting yourself from those who are not good for you. The people who make you feel invalidated and dismissed. They could be your closest friend or a family member. If they can't create a safe place for you or, at the very least, not create an unsafe place, counsellors, therapists, and healers will advise you to let go of these relationships. They are zapping your energy. This creates a huge amount of grief and sadness. However, the focus for healing must be on self-care and self-protection. Setting boundaries is a step to taking back power and to begin to feel less helpless, more empowered, and re-energised.

New people will begin to be drawn to you. You will attract the right people into your life—people who will see and hear you. People who see your resilience and your strength. These people are sacred connections. I found a tribe of women and men to hold me close, offer me comfort, and teach me that I am enough. I am brave. And so are you. We are all worthy of love and joy and peace.

There are so many people, teachers, workshops, modes of healing, and therapies that I have included in my healing journey. The most important thing is that any counsellor or healer is gentle and follows your lead. That they create a place where you feel safe and that they only move in your area of comfort so that you are growing and healing at your pace. If you open yourself up to the possibility of healing, you will attract light givers and you will heal. The wounds and scars may remain, but you and your life can grow around those wounds.

In *The Body Keeps the Score*, Bessel van der Kolk writes, "After trauma the world is experienced with a different nervous system" (2014). Our nervous system is highly reactive. Our body seems to handle less stimuli and continues to feel trauma. It can also exacerbate chronic pain conditions. We need to learn to soothe the nervous system.

Just recently, I discovered that my changed concept of time is a symptom of complex trauma. I had always been a long-term planner. A person who was future-focused. I thought my focus on the present was due to my mindfulness practice, and possibly some of it is. However, I do have a foreshortened sense of the future and that comes from overwhelming amounts of grief and trauma. Mindfulness practice helps turn the present focus into a positive, joyful practice. It helps you connect with today.

For me, connection allowed me to feel safe in my grief and gave me a place to let go.

Nothing is simple, and I am not going to paint a pretty picture here. Suicide is complicated at any time. Add domestic abuse and families who are estranged, and it gets a whole lot more complex.

I am a strong believer in healing through connection. Isolation and loneliness break our hearts. Connection is an energy giver. Being a part of several healthy communities has aided my healing. I think anyone having a difficult time might find it helpful to join community groups: charity groups, meditation groups, sports clubs, or groups that interest you. Volunteer if you can. Find people who are givers, who are kind. You don't have to share your story. Just being able to feel a part of a community is a start. In time, you may meet like-minded and like-hearted people. Finding people who have similar experiences or interests and passions can be helpful as you are able to really empathise with each other. I have made some very strong connections, had some incredibly deep and meaningful conversations, and made some of my closest friends through common interest groups or volunteering.

I believe in therapy but also in finding the right therapy and therapist for you: a trauma-informed therapist. I have been blessed with empathetic, kind, gentle therapists, counsellors, and social workers who also offered me guidance and were a little firm when I needed it. I believe you need to feel safe and comfortable with your therapist. I believe you need to feel understood, and if your instinct tells you the relationship is not right, then move on. If you are not growing or healing, move on.

I have benefited greatly from regular visits to my kinesiologist who seems to know how to offer me strength, light, and a connection with self. She is able to rebalance my energy and bring my nervous system back to homeostasis, rebuilding trust in myself and my intuition.

Daily journaling is a go to for me to deal with rumination, sorting out my thoughts and emotional regulation. Getting it down on paper, even if you never revisit it again is therapeutic.

Meditation and living a mindful life have been a giant part of my healing journey. Breathwork is a huge part of that. It has brought kind, healing people into my life who have taught me many things. One of the benefits of mindfulness is learning to pause. The more we practise meditation, the longer the pause becomes. We get to choose to respond rather than to react. And so when we are triggered, angered, frustrated, or overwhelmed, or any type of emotion arises, we pause and make a choice, then respond. This is always an ongoing work in progress.

Mindfulness has also allowed me greater access to connect to myself, to others, and to the greater universe. Getting out into nature is healing.

Yoga is moving meditation for me. A peaceful place even during chaos and storms. A gentle yoga class can soothe the nervous system and be calming. Learning to be fully present and doing a class with closed eyes is incredibly self-soothing.

Movement is a powerful tool. Children instinctively rock themselves to self-soothe. Shaking our bodies can help rebalance our energies. Stand up and shake your hands and feet, then shake your whole body. Release any negative energy and invite in the positive energy.

One of my most joyous memories is dancing at sunrise with my babies, kissing their chubby faces and listening to their laughter. Dancing boosts your mood and increases your vitality. Every morning put on a happy song and dance.

LESSONS I HAVE LEARNED:

- Rest and recover:
    - Get out into nature. Walk by a river, the ocean, or a field of flowers.
    - Connect and savour the beauty around you.
    - Move your body.
    - Focus on what you love and what you are grateful for.
    - Pay attention to the little things, like a stranger who passed you and smiled, the sun shining on your back, a baby giggling, art, or music.
    - Consider adopting a pet. We adopted a rescue kitten. He has brought a huge amount of joy, cuddles, and love. He definitely reduces anxiety with his presence.
    - Start a journal. Pour your thoughts out. Use your voice, even if no one hears you. Even if you burn those pages, it is healing.

SIXTEEN

The Tortoise and the Hare

SLOW AND STEADY

The whole world
Is a very narrow bridge
and the main thing is not to be paralysed by your fear
—Rabbi Nachman

I was truly in fight, flight, and freeze when leaving my relationship, and the constant, ongoing post-separation attacks kept me in a hypervigilant state. I endured seven years of post-separation abuse. Seven years of learning to quiet the hypervigilance, learning to breathe, learning to calm the panic. Seven years of increasing the size of the pause, finding moments of flow, and finding connection. This has helped me feel empowered and find my way back to peace and joy.

Healing includes taking back your power. This may include very practical steps to obtain skills to feel more empowered. Often people in control or abuse situations need to know where to find resources and help. The more access we give to the resources, the easier it is to leave, to survive, and to thrive. Among others, I needed to learn to set boundaries, to learn everyday financial skills like how to do my taxes, and how to work within the court system.

Brave and Afraid.
Healed and Healing.

Be patient with yourself and be patient with the process. Accept where you are. Learn to let all things be as they are. Know that healing and change includes grieving: grieving love lost, friends lost, innocence lost, losing yourself, as well as, often, the cost to health and home and belongings. Expect waves of pain, panic, sadness, and despair.

Healing also includes discovering strength you didn't know you had and the courage to keep going and fight on, meeting extraordinary, inspiring people, each of whom will teach you something. Some days will be yours to help others, and some days it will be others to help you. Some days, I am the hope-holder, and other days, I have the need for someone to hold my hope for me. To shine the light. There is grief and heartache, but there is much joy and discovery, meaning and purpose, peace and connectivity.

Healing is an ongoing journey of living and learning. There are days when I feel empowered, connected, and calm and think I am winning at life. I have beaten the trauma. I am doing tremendously well. I am ready to get a tattoo: "I am the storm." And then, the very next day, there will be a trigger, and I will be back to self-soothing. Rocking, palms on chest, breathing and counting, in and out, in and out. I will be on the phone with my social worker or friends and booking an appointment with my kinesiologist. I feel like I am all the way back to the beginning. On reflection, I am not. I have grown. I know what I need. I reach inward and outward for help. I am soon calm, connected, and empowered again. This is a journey. These cycles are natural and to be expected. The more we fight them, the more the anxiety, fear, and sadness envelopes us. Instead, we need to accept what comes and acknowledge all we have been through. Welcome the emotion in. Have compassion for yourself. Offer shelter and patience, not judgement. The cycles get shorter.

The secrecy and stigma need to be lifted for a light to shine on perpetrators' behaviour. It is not a victim's shame to hold. It is time we talk about these issues and realise that as a society, as a community, we can proactively make a difference. Hold the perpetrator accountable and empower those people who may be taken advantage of. Silence is power and control for the perpetrator. Let's change that.

Communication is power.

Knowledge is power.

Connection is power.

LESSONS LEARNED

- Transparency
    - Financial institutions, insurance brokers, financial advisors, bank managers, and lawyers can do more. They are beginning to do more. Any time a financial consultant is asked for advice or help, or each time they meet with a person who is part of a couple, they should be insisting on transparency and on seeing both or all of the members of the partnership. Each party should understand the decisions being made and agree to each. Each party should be updated on changes made. Each person should have access to online portals and information.
- Repentance and repair
    - After much pain, tears, wrestling, and hoping for the alternative, I choose to accept there will be no repentance and repair process with my and my children's abuser and instead live knowing we have peace, purpose, and joy.
    - Repair only works where there is behaviour change.
- Choose your own ending—Rise
    - This book is how I chose to write my own ending—of this part of my story.
    - Each of us gets to take our power back. Slowly. Purposefully. Reach out for all the resources available and rebuild. Take your

time. Find yourself again. We can choose how to live our lives with meaning, gratitude, and hope.
- Healing is a journey.
    - You can choose to heal. You can choose joy, love, and peace.
- Start living today.
    - You can feel joy and peace and love as you heal. Don't wait for the perfect time. Gratitude helps us focus on what we have and reminds us that we are enough as we are. Is there one thing you can be grateful for today?
- There are many forms of healing work that survivors find helpful.
    - I have found yoga (especially with a trauma-informed teacher), breath work, meditation, mindfulness, inner-child work, vagus nerve work, kinesiology, and trauma-informed therapy all helpful.
- Let yourself heal as you need to with no time limit.
    - Let things be as they are. Accept and let your healing be.
    - Find peace, and then find your wings to fly.

AUSTRALIAN RESOURCES

1800 Respect

a 24/7 national helpline for sexual, domestic, and family violence

Phone: 1800 737 732

Website: https://www.1800respect.org.au

Beyond Blue

offers mental health support

Phone: 1300 22 4636

Website: https://www.beyondblue.org.au

inTouch Multicultural Centre Against Family Violence

provides services, programs, and responses to family violence in migrant and refugee communities

Phone: 1800 755 988

Website: https://intouch.org.au

Kids Helpline

24/7 online and phone counselling service for young people

Phone: 1800 55 1800

https://kidshelpline.com.au

Lifeline Australia
a crisis support line
Phone: 13 11 14
Website: https://www.lifeline.org.au

The Orange Door
help for people who are experiencing family violence or who need support with the care and wellbeing of children and young people
Website: https://orangedoor.vic.gov.au/contact

Safe Steps
Victoria's 24/7 Family and Domestic Violence Support Response Centre
Phone: 1800 015 188
Website: https://www.safesteps.org.au/about-us/contact-us

FINANCIAL ABUSE RESOURCES

Centre for Women's Economic Safety
provides financial abuse resources
Website: https://financialsafety.org.au

National Debt Helpline
access to financial counsellors
Website: https://ndh.org.au
Phone: 1800 007 007

GLOSSARY

Alienation: Isolating you from your friends and family.

Boundaries: The limits and rules we set for ourselves in relationships. For example, a healthy boundary might be around how much information we choose to share about ourselves. Unhealthy boundaries include oversharing personal information or avoiding intimacy and close relationships.

Coercive Control: A repeated pattern of control and dominance over a partner to restrict their freedom and autonomy. Control can include verbal, economic, psychological, as well as sexual and physical violence. This often escalates in danger when the survivor tries to leave, resulting in continued post-separation abuse (including systems abuse). Coercive control is an underlying dynamic in intimate partner violence.

Control: Using tactics to influence another persons agency or behaviour

Control Tactics: Rules are put in place early with consequences for stepping outside of them.

DARVO: An acronym for "deny, attack, and reverse victim and offender," where the abuser turns the story around and becomes the victim.

Economic Abuse: Includes financial abuse and is a serious form of domestic and family violence that occurs when an abuser uses money and resources as a means to gain power and to control their partner or family member.

Financial Abuse: Withholding or mismanaging financial resources and support to maintain power and dependence.

Flying Monkeys: A term given to the active helpers of the narcissist.

Gaslighting: The person deliberately deceives you and manipulates the truth and your thoughts and feelings, making you think you are remembering things wrong or misinterpreting events.

Grey Rock Communication: Only communicating the facts and essentials in communications without emotion or courtesies, making yourself uninteresting.

Grooming: Behaviours used towards the victim, family support, and friends to manipulate and charm people and get access to people and resources.

Harassment: Using persistent and frightening tactics to control and intimidate the victim.

Intimidation: The act of frightening someone eg threatening or glaring in a way that you know they mean to hurt you.

Intimate Partner Violence (IPV): "Any behaviour within an intimate relationship (current or previous) that causes physical, sexual or psychological harm" (Australian Institute of Health and Welfare, 2023).

Isolation: Intentionally damaging the victim's relationships with family, friends, and support networks. Spreading rumours, destroying reputations, and compromising support systems.

Legal Abuse: Exploiting the legal system to gain power and control over the victim.

Manipulation: To behave in a way that is unfair to your own advantage.

Narcissistic Personality Disorder: Narcissism trait is on a spectrum. Narcissistic personality disorder or pathological narcissism is the far extreme and includes the extreme manifestations of a strong desire for admiration, an inflated self-image, and a lack of empathy. Relationships are transactional for narcissists. It helps them achieve something, build their self-esteem, and develop their ego.

Personality Disorders: Atypical ways of thinking about oneself and relating to other people are grouped into three clusters: A, B, and C. Cluster B disorders are marked by inappropriate, volatile emotionality and often unpredictable behaviour. The disorders in Cluster B are antisocial personality disorder, borderline personality disorder, histrionic personality disorder, and narcissistic personality disorder.

Post-Separation Abuse: The abuse that continues, and often escalates, after the end of a relationship. Often becoming all pervasive for the healthy parent, post-separation abuse is used to control, hurt, and create fear for the safe parent. Post-separation abuse is coercive control.

Projection: Displacing one's feelings onto a different person, animal, or object. The term is most commonly used to describe defensive projection—attributing one's own unacceptable urges to another.

Spiritual/Religious Abuse: Includes causing distress and isolation using members of an organisation, using your own beliefs against you to keep power over you.

Stalking: Phone calls all day, every day, and/or surveillance.

Trauma Bonding: A deep emotional attachment to someone who has harmed us, often caused by a repeated cycle of love and rewards followed by threats, abuse, and punishment.

Yellow Rock Communication: The recommended communication style with the narcissistic abuser you are having to communicate with. It involves communicating facts and staying on topic but being courteous as if always imagining you are being overheard by a court official judging you, having prepared responses, being focused, and not allowing yourself to be baited into any other communication *(Swithin,n.d.)*.

KEY LESSONS TO SHARE

1. All abuse is abuse. All abuse is damaging. All abuse can lead to consequences that are life-changing, disempowering, and trauma-inducing.

2. Abuse happens in all communities.

3. Remember that coercive control is a pattern of behaviour, not isolated behaviour. Signs that you or someone you know are experiencing coercive control include:

   - Feeling unsafe around that person and being unsure why.
   - Feeling like you cannot express your thoughts or emotions to that person or others for fear of the consequences.
   - Negative consequences for not behaving the way that person wants you to behave, dress, or speak.
   - Attempts to isolate you from your friends, family, or work.
   - Attempts to control your income or control your financial freedom.
   - Feeling confused by their behaviour, e.g. threatening behaviour and then alternating it with rewarding behaviour, attempting to make you feel guilty.
   - Monitoring your movements.
   - Constantly checking up on you.
   - Manipulating you into unwanted sexual acts.

- Calling you names and belittling you.

4. Trust your gut. Listen to your inner voice- your inner wisdom. Your intuition is your superpower. Watch people's actions. See them.

5. Children are victims in their own right. Children's voices need to be heard.

6. Listen, acknowledge, and support when people come forward. Believe victim-survivors when they tell you their story.

7. If it is safe, we must try to be upstanders.

8. Reach out. Let people in.

9. Feel your emotions. "Feel it to heal it."

10. Watch for red flags.

    - Those tiny red flags that get bigger until they are screaming in your face.
    - These are small signals we often miss. For example, when you feel you are not safe to say something or do something or are "walking on eggshells."

11. Pay attention to green flags.

    - Live with an open heart and allow yourself to trust again. Choose to be happy, connected, and fulfilled.
    - Relationships with green flags make you feel safe, calm, and seen. Green flags include open communication, emotional and financial transparency, feeling like you

both have a voice and feel supported.
- You feel you can be your true self—your authentic self.
- Being able to make mistakes and still feel safe within your relationship.

12. Understand the nervous system's traffic lights.

    - The sympathetic nervous system is the yellow light of the nervous system. Most of us live here unknowingly. That is because most of us are highly stressed, hyper-aroused, and hypervigilant. We are often triggered easily. We are in flight-or-fight mode—stress biological mode. We are looking out for danger, ready for action.
    - Sometimes we are in danger overload—a red traffic light. Our parasympathetic nervous system is overactive, and our freeze mode is activated.
    - The green traffic light is the optimal connector. This is when our ventral vagal nerve is stimulated. This activates creativity, love, and connection. This occurs when we feel safe and secure.
    - We can calm the nervous system, and move toward the green light.

13. Know the importance of setting up boundaries.

14. Provide safety and offer support to victims.

    - Offer immediate safe housing and financial aid.
    - Offer comfort, compassion, and kindness.
    - Offer skills training in feeling empowered, finances,

assertive language, and legal aid.
- Offer safe places to share stories and connect.
- Offer trauma-informed counselling and alternative healing modalities.

15. Throughout this book, we have mentioned what not to say to trauma survivors. We know it is easy to get it wrong unintentionally. Most people are doing their best. However, here is a cheat sheet to guide you.

    - What NOT to say:
        - We didn't see it.
        - You are overreacting.
        - I know how you feel.
        - We have to walk on eggshells around you.
        - Move on.
        - Let go.
        - Forgive.
        - Don't hold a grudge.
        - We have to stay neutral.
        - There are two sides to every story.
    - Words of affirmation, acknowledgement, and connection include:
        - I hear you.
        - I believe you.
        - I've got you.
        - What do you need?
        - I'm listening.
        - Can I sit with you?
        - How do you feel?
        - How can I support you?

16. Advocate for system change.

    - Financial institutions and advisors are part of the solution. They can choose to work to empower all partners in a relationship to have transparent financial relationships. They can ensure all partners in the relationship are fully informed (and educated) at all stages of decision-making and changes in finances.
    - Lawyers and judges can be held accountable for the ways they behave in the courtroom by the systems that place them there. A lawyer shouting at an abused woman and calling her a liar is not OK. How does no one step up and call that behaviour out?

17. Repentance and repair.

    - Sometimes we have to accept there won't be repentance and repair.
    - Repentance and repair only works where there is behaviour change.

18. Choose your own ending.

    - We can choose how we show up in the world.
    - As Brené Brown says in her 2015 book *Rising Strong*, "Our job is not to deny the story, but to defy the ending—to rise strong, recognize [sic] our story, and rumble with the truth until we get to a place where we think, Yes. This is what happened. And I will choose how the story ends."
    - Each of us gets to take our power back. Slowly. Purposefully. Reach out for all the resources available

and rebuild. Take your time. Find yourself again. We can choose how to live our lives with meaning, gratitude, and hope.

19. Healing is a journey. You can choose to heal. You can choose joy and love and peace.

    - Start living today. You can feel joy and peace and love as you heal. Don't wait for the perfect time.

20. There are many forms of healing.

    - There are many forms of healing work that survivors find helpful. Try different modalities and see what resonates for you.
    - Let yourself heal with no time limit. Let things be as they are. More compassion and curiosity, less judgement.
      o Breathwork is healing. One of the biggest healing mechanisms is our breath. Learn to come home to yourself.
      o Try this breath-grounding exercise:
        - Put your hand over the centre of your chest.
        - Breathe in slowly through your nose, hold, and breathe out slowly through your mouth.
        - Repeat three times.
        - If it is comfortable to do so, close your eyes while you do this.
        - Repeat throughout the day.
      o Try this meta (loving kindness) exercise:
        o What I wish for all of us:
        o Say these words to yourself, with closed

eyes if possible.
  - Repeat three times.
  - May I be happy.
  - May I be safe.
  - May I be loved.
  - May I live with ease and grace and an open heart.
- Healing requires rest. Be kind to yourself. Listen to your body. Rest and heal.

REFERENCES

ABC News. (2021, January 25). "Hear me now": Australian of the Year Grace Tame's powerful speech in full. [YouTube]. https://www.youtube.com/watch?v=LJmwOTfjn9U

ABS Personal Safety Survey: Additional Analysis on Relationship and Sex of Perpetrator. (n.d.). https://violenceagainstwomenandchildren.wordpress.com/wp-content/uploads/2015/07/abs-personal-safety-survey-victim-perpetrator-sex-and-relationship6.pdf

ANROWS Institute. (2023). *Attitudes Matter: The 2021 National Community Attitudes Towards Violence Against Women Survey.* Findings for Australia (Research report 02/2023).

Australian Bureau of Statistics. (2016). *Personal Safety, Australia.* https://www.abs.gov.au/statistics/people/crime-and-justice/personal-safety-australia/2016

Australian Bureau of Statistics. (2023, March 22). *Nearly 1 in 200 People Homeless on Census Night in 2021.* [Media Release]. https://www.abs.gov.au/media-centre/media-releases/nearly-1-200-people-homeless-census-night-2021

Australian Bureau of Statistics (22 November 2023), *1 in 5 Australians have experienced partner violence or abuse*, ABS Website, accessed 20 February 2025.

Borderline Personality Disorder. (2023, September 1). *Advancing Mental Health in America*. https://www.adamhscc.org/resources/facts-about-mental-illness/borderline-personality-disorder

Brown, B. (2015). *Rising Strong: The Reckoning. The Rumble. The Revolution*. Random House.

Carlisle, E., Coumarelos, C., Minter, K., & Lohmeyer, B. (2022). *"It Depends on What the Definition of Domestic Violence Is": How Young Australians Conceptualise Domestic Violence and Abuse*. ANROWS Institute. https://www.anrows.org.au/publication/it-depends-on-what-the-definition-of-domestic-violence-is-how-young-people-conceptualise-domestic-violence-and-abuse/

Coercive Control. (2020). https://dcj.nsw.gov.au/documents/children-and-families/family-domestic-and-sexual-violence/domestic-and-family-violence-/domestic-violence-discussion-paper-coercive-control.pdf

Coercive Control, Non-Physical Violence and Relationship Red Flags. (n.d.). Respect Victoria. https://www.respectvictoria.vic.gov.au/coercive-control-non-physical-violence-and-relationship-red-flags

Coumarelos, C., Weeks, N., Bernstein, S., Roberts, N., Honey, N., Minter, K., & Carlisle, E. (2023). *Attitudes Matter: The 2021 National Community Attitudes towards Violence against Women Survey (NCAS), Findings for Australia*. Australia National Research Organisation for Women's Safety. https://www.anrows.org.au/publication/attitudes-matter-the-2021-national-community-attitudes-towards-violence-against-women-survey-ncas-findings-for-australia/ *CWES—Centre for Women's Economic Safety.* (n.d.). https://cwes.org.au

Doyle, G. (2020). *Untamed: Stop Pleasing, Start Living.* Penguin-Random House.

Experience of Family Violence Among People Who Suicided, Victoria 2009-2016.

(2024). Coroners Court of Victoria. https://www.coronerscourt.vic.gov.au/sites/defaultfiles/2024-09/Coroners%20Court%20of%20Victoria%20Experience%20of%20family%20violence%20among%20people%20who%20suicided%202009-20016.pdf

Harsey, S., & Freyd, J. J. (2020). Deny, Attack, and Reverse Victim and Offender (DARVO): What Is the Influence on Perceived Perpetrator and Victim Credibility? *Journal of Aggression, Maltreatment & Trauma,* 29(8), 897-916. https://doi.org/10.1080/10926771.2020.1774695

Hill, J. (2019). *See What You Made Me Do.* Black Inc.

Intimate Partner Violence. (n.d.). Australian Institute of Health and Welfare. https://www.aihw.gov.au/family-domestic-and-sexual-violence/types-of-violence/intimate-partner-violence

Katz, E. (2023). *Understanding Coercive Control and its Impacts on Children.* Ministry of Social and Family Development. https://www.msf.gov.sg/docs/default-source/msf-event/dr-emma-katz---keynote-address-2.pdf?sfvrsn=3bb30dbc_3#:~:text=Coercive%20control%20involves%20situations%20where

Mayo Clinic. (2023, April 6). *Narcissistic Personality*

Disorder. Mayo Clinic. https://www.mayoclinic.org/diseases-conditions/narcissistic-personality-disorder/symptoms-causes/syc-20366662

Minter, K., Carlisle, E., & Coumarelos, C. (2021). *"Chuck Her on a Lie Detector": Investigating Australians' Mistrust in Women's Reports of Sexual Assault*. ANROWS Institute. nexlec.com

National Council of Jewish Women in Australia. (2020). *Unchain my Heart—The Story of Gett and Agunah*. https://www.ncjwa.org.au/unchain-my-heart-the-story-of-gett-and-agunah/

New South Wales Domestic Violence Death Review Team. *(2022). Report 2019-2021*. https://apo.org.au/organisation/174806, accessed 20 February 2025.

New South Wales Government. (n.d.). *First Print Crimes Legislation Amendment (Coercive Control) Bill 2022 Explanatory Note Overview of Bill*. https://legislation.nsw.gov.au/view/pdf/bill/130050ae-893f-42cd-95e5-b68d5695e29d

Our Watch. (2021). *Change the Story: A Shared Framework for the Primary Prevention of Violence Against Women in Australia* (2nd ed.). whlm.org.au

Personality Disorders. (2023, July 12). Psychology Today. https://www.psychologytoday.com/us/basics/personality-disorders

Ramani, D. (2024). *It's Not You: How to Identify and Heal from Narcissistic People*. Vermilion-Mass Market.

Ruttenberg, D. (2022). *On Repentance and Repair: Making Amends in an Unapologetic World*. Beacon Press.

Safe Steps. (2014). Family Violence Myths & Facts. Safe Steps Family Violence Response Centre. https://www.safesteps.org.au/understanding-family-violence/family-violence-myths-facts/

Swthin, T. (n.d.). Implementing Yellow Rock Communication When Co-Parenting with a Narcissist. One Mom's Battle. https://www.onemomsbattle.com/blog/implementing-yellowrock-communication-when-co-parenting-with-anarcissist

Stark, E. (2007). *Coercive Control: How Men Entrap Women in Personal Life*. Oxford University Press.

Van der Kolk, B. (2014). *The Body Keeps the Score: Brain, Mind, and Body in the Healing of Trauma*. Viking Press.

WIRE. (2018, December 6). *What is Financial Abuse?* WIRE. https://www.wire.org.au/financial-abuse/

SOURCES FOR EPIGRAPHS AND QUOTES

Campbell, J. (1949). *The Hero with a Thousand Faces*. Pantheon Books.

Fanon, F. (1963). *The Wretched of the Earth*. Grove Press.

Morrison, T. (1987). *Beloved*. Alfred A. Knopf.

Nachman of Bratslav. (n.d.). The Narrow Bridge. Breslov Research Institute. https://breslov.org/the-narrow-bridge/

Obama, M. (2018). *Becoming*. Crown Publishers.

Polley, S. (Director) (2022) Women Talking. [Film] Hear/Say Productions.

Roosevelt, T. (1910). Citizenship in a Republic. The Works of

Theodore Roosevelt (Vol. 19, pp. 267-286). Scribner's Sons.

Todd, H. M. (1911, September). Bread for all, and roses too. *The American Magazine*.

Wiesel, E. (2017). Elie Wiesel Acceptance Speech. NobelPrize.org.

https://www.nobelprize.org/prizes/peace/1986/wiesel/acceptance-speech/

Wittgenstein, L. (1922). *Tractatus Logico-Philosophicus*. Routledge & Kegan Paul, London.

www.ingramcontent.com/pod-product-compliance
Lightning Source LLC
Chambersburg PA
CBHW032039200426
43209CB00049B/30